OTHER BOOKS BY TRAILER LIFE

An RVer's Annual: The Best of Trailer Life and Motorhome
Edited by Rena Copperman

This collector's edition of the best travel, technical, personality, and feature articles from past issues of the magazines, acknowledged as the leading publications in the RV field, is topped off with a special "Constitution" feature, recalling the recent nationwide anniversary celebration in prose and pictures. Beautiful four-color photos throughout . . . a great gift idea.
8½×11, 208 pages
$15.95 ISBN: 0-934798-21-4

Full-time RVing: A Complete Guide to Life on the Open Road
Bill and Jan Moeller

The answers to all the questions anyone who dreams of traveling full time in an RV may have can be found in this remarkable new source book. *Full-time RVing* takes the mystery out of fulltiming and makes it possible to fully enjoy this once-in-a-lifetime experience.
7¼×9¼, 352 pages
$14.95 ISBN: 0-934798-14-1

RX for RV Performance & Mileage
John Geraghty and Bill Estes

In 32 chapters, this book covers everything an owner must know about how an engine (particularly a V-8) works, vehicle maintenance, propane and diesel as alternative fuels, eliminating engine "ping," improving exhaust systems and fuel economy, and much more.
7¾×9¼, 359 pages
$14.95 ISBN: 0-934798-08-0

The Good Sam RV Cookbook
Edited by Beverly Edwards and the editors of *Trailer Life*

Over 250 easy and delicious recipes, including 78 prize-winners from Good Sam Samboree cook-offs around the country. Also contains tips, ideas, and suggestions to help you get the most from your RV galley.
7¼×9¼, 252 pages
$14.95 ISBN: 0-934798-17-6

These books are available at fine bookstores everywhere. Or, you may order directly from Trailer Life. For each book ordered, simply send us the name of the book, the price, plus $2 per book for shipping and handling (California residents please add 6½% sales tax). Mail to:

Trailer Life Books, P.O. Box 4500, Agoura, CA 91301

You may call our Customer Service representatives if you wish to charge your order or if you want more information. Please phone, toll-free, Monday through Friday, 7:00 A.M. to 6:00 P.M.; Saturday, 7:30 A.M. to 12:30 P.M. Pacific Time, **1-800-234-3450.**

RVing America's Backroads:

Kenneth W. Dahse

With photographs by Buddy Mays

…Light-hearted I take to the open road,
Healthy, free, the world before me,
The long brown path before me leading
wherever I choose.

Walt Whitman, *Song of the Open Road*

Trailer Life Books
Agoura, California

DEDICATION

To Linda, my wife and friend, for all she has done, and to my parents, William and Dorothy, for always being there when I needed them.

With special thanks to Rena Copperman, my editor, for all her assistance and patience.

Trailer Life Book Division

President: Richard Rouse
Vice President/General Manager: Ted Binder
Vice President/Publisher, Book Division: Michael Schneider
General Manager, Book Division: Rena Copperman
Assistant Manager, Book Division: Cindy Lang

Cover design: Bob Schroeder
Color consultant: almazangraphics
Interior design: David Fuller/Robert S. Tinnon
Production manager: Rena Copperman
Production coordinator: Robert S. Tinnon
Editorial assistant: Judi Lazarus
Special contributor: Stephanie Boyle
Indexer: Barbara Wurf
Maps: EarthSurface Graphics
Color separations: Western Laser Graphics

All photographs are Buddy Mays's unless otherwise credited.
Cover photograph by: Dennis Hallinan, FPG, New York

This book was set in ITC Garamond Book by Andresen Typographics and printed on 60-pound Shoreweb Gloss by R.R. Donnelley and Sons in Willard, Ohio.

ISBN 0-934798-24-9

Library of Congress Cataloging-in-Publication Data

Dahse, Kenneth W., 1949-
    RVing America's backroads: New York.

    Includes index.
    1. Automobiles—New York (State)—Touring.   2. Recreational vehicles—New York (State)   3. New York (State)—Description and travel—1981–   —Guide-books.   I.   Title.
GV1024.D34   1989   917.47   88-24799
ISBN 0-934798-24-9

Contents

Preface

I have traveled and written about New York for many years. Conducting the research necessary to produce this book was a rewarding experience and the culmination of all my travels.

To other RVers planning to tour the state, I must assure you that as I traveled throughout the state I experienced no difficulty in locating a campground. New York has more campsites per square mile of land area than any of the other forty-nine states (a total of 48,000 sites). Most of the larger public campgrounds have restrooms, showers, dumping stations, and a few have hookups. Most of the private campgrounds offer complete amenities. When planning your stops it's best to consult your *Trailer Life Campground & Services Directory.*

Also, unless otherwise indicated in these tours, there aren't any limitations on recreational vehicles or their sizes. This allows all RVers to enjoy the diversity of New York's land and people, offering an infinite amount of experiences and thousands of miles of backroads to explore.

In the course of writing and traveling, I had a great amount of help. A heartfelt thanks to the members of the state's Department of Environmental Conservation and the Department of Commerce; the local chambers of commerce; and most importantly, the residents of New York, who were always willing to offer their friendship and knowledge. Additional thank yous to Thomas A. Breslin and Tony Ingraham of the New York State Office of Parks, Recreation, and Historic Preservation, and of course to Buddy Mays, photographer without peer, whose pictures illuminate and amplify the text so perfectly.

We must also not forget the great debt we all owe to the early conservationists and the foresighted politicians who listened to them. They were the ones who persevered and, because of their tenacity, preserved millions of acres of land for us and future generations to enjoy. The battle still rages, and supporting our contemporary conservationists will help insure that New York's beauty will remain a treasure for all future backroads travelers to enjoy.

NEW YORK

New York is known as the Empire State and rightly so; it is a land rich in history, beauty, and conflict. New York was once ruled by the powerful Iroquois Indian Confederacy, an empire in its own right, which held the balance of power between the French and British while they fought for hegemony of the continent.

The state is a vast economic power, both culturally and ethnically diverse, with an expansive topography of mountains, wild rivers, farmland, and woodland wilderness. It ranks thirtieth in size, covering 49,576 square miles, but has the largest park in the lower forty-eight states, one that not only dwarfs Wyoming's Yellowstone National Park, but is also larger than several bordering states.

The Adirondack State Park Forest Preserve lies in the eastern section of New York State and consists of over 6 million acres of land. It encompasses 5 chains of mountains; over 2,000 lakes; numerous wild rivers; and is home to black bear, deer, coyote, loon, bobcat, and many other species, including 125,000 year-round residents scattered in (mostly) small villages throughout the region. The park, like Catskill State Park to the south, is not a contiguous wilderness, but is interspersed with development and has hundreds of miles of backroads for RVers to experience.

Within its boundaries are over a million acres of wilderness land with miles of trails, rugged peaks, lakes, and rivers for exploration. The park also has historic sites and towns and exciting resort areas. Famous writers, such as James Fenimore Cooper and Ned Buntline, glorified the Adirondacks. Cooper used the area as a setting for some of his novels, most notably The Last of the Mohicans.

South of the Adirondacks lies the historic Hudson River Valley, which has been compared to Germany's Rhine region. And its many "great estates," wineries, picturesque villages, and lush farmland add credence to that analogy. It is here America's own aristocracy of Roosevelts, Vanderbilts, and Rockefellers made their homes; now their estates are open for public viewing.

The western section of New York includes the world-renown Finger Lakes region, comprised of eleven fingerlike lakes, impressive waterfalls, deep gorges, and vineyards that support over forty wineries. Pushing even further west, that Western Frontier is home to two Indian reservations and the proud descendants of the Seneca Nation. The region is rich in cultural complexity and scenic beauty, including Letchworth State Park, which has been called the "Grand Canyon of the East." This area is also home to a thriving Amish farming community. They migrated from Ohio and turned the once-depressed farmlands into prosperous entities with nineteenth-century farming methods, devoid of modern conveniences and expenses.

Lake George-Champlain Historic Trail

Ever since I arrived to a state of manhood and acquainted myself to the general history of mankind, I felt a sincere passion for liberty.

Ethan Allen,
April, 1775

It was with fond memories that I began my tour of the Lake George-Champlain Historic Trail. This beautiful region lies along the eastern boundary of Adirondack State Park in northeastern New York, bordered on the west by Vermont. I have been visiting parts of the area since childhood and was looking forward to returning to old attractions and discovering new ones.

Lake George, thirty-two miles long, is known as the Queen of the Adirondack Lakes because of its superb scenery and crystal-clear water; it is not uncommon to be able to see the bottom at depths of twenty to thirty feet. Lake George is steeped in history; it has witnessed Indian battles, colonial wars, the clash of empires, and the War of Independence.

Tour **1** *156 miles*
Side trip to Pharaoh Lakes Wilderness, 25 miles

LAKE GEORGE VILLAGE • LAKE GEORGE SCENIC DRIVE • ROGERS' ROCK • TICONDEROGA • CROWN POINT • ESSEX • AUSABLE CHASM • LAKE CHAMPLAIN

Starting Point: Lake George Village

I planned to begin my tour at Lake George Village (population, 1,000). Some people might consider the area too touristy and overdeveloped, but I find it has much to offer. There are numerous restaurants, shops, a beautiful million-dollar beach, museums, and enough activities for every member of the family to find something of interest.

On Prospect Mountain

On the way into Lake George Village, I took a scenic ride on Prospect Mountain State Parkway, off US Highway 9, a 5½-mile paved toll road up Prospect Mountain, with a vertical rise of 1,530 feet, a summit elevation of 2,030 feet, and a maximum grade of 9 percent. The drive is easy enough for the largest motorhome, and there's a parking area for 800 cars just below the summit. There are three overlooks on the highway, with each view more expansive than the last. To my surprise, I passed a road gang, something I thought only existed in the Old South. I asked a ranger about it. "Don't be concerned 'bout them," he smiled. "They aren't dangerous, just minor criminals, and they don't want to go anyplace. They have it real easy. The state feeds, clothes, and houses them, and lets them enjoy a day in the sun."

Being somewhat reassured, I hopped on the free shuttle bus at the parking lot and rode to the summit to be rewarded with a spectacular panorama. I could see the lake weaving in and around the mountains, the vast wilderness of the Adirondacks spreading westward, the Green Mountains of Vermont to the east, and below, Lake George Village. On a clear day, you might see a hundred miles in every direction.

At one time there was a Prospect Mountain House, catering to wealthy vacationers and day visitors. A stay at the house was $3 a day including meals, a mighty sum considering the average wage at the time was $3 a week. Built in the 1870s by Dr. James Ferguson, a retired Glens Falls physi-

Ausable Chasm.
The pristine beauty of the Champlain Valley's Ausable Chasm has enchanted visitors since the 1870s. The spectacular gorge can be viewed on foot or by boat.

cian and local entrepreneur, it was destroyed by a forest fire in 1880. The hotel was rebuilt, only to burn down again.

Visitors had to come up to the hotel on foot or in horse-drawn carriages before a 7,392-foot cable railroad was built at a cost of $110,000 in 1895. The fifty-cent trip from Lake George Village ran every half hour. After only eight years the line ceased operations; the rails were eventually used for scrap during World War I. Today, all remnants of the hotel are gone, save one bull wheel from the railroad. Prospect Mountain is now a state-owned picnic and recreation area, and I highly recommend a visit.

I drove down the mountain enjoying the views from a different perspective but anxious to park so I could grab a bite to eat. Lake George Village can satisfy most culinary tastes with its variety of restaurants. I, however, chose my traditional Lake George fare—a mundane but delicious submarine sandwich at Mike's Subs. I pulled my rig into the parking area by the docks and ate my lunch at the water's edge, enjoying the views of the lake, cruise ships in front of me and Fort William Henry behind me.

View from the Top.
On a clear day the view of Lake George and Lake George Village from the top of nearby Prospect Mountain can be breathtaking.

Remembrance of Colonial Days

Fort William Henry, standing proudly on its promontory overlooking southern Lake George, was built in 1755 and patronizingly named after two of King George's nephews. Major General William Johnson, the British superintendent-general of Indian affairs in North America, ordered its construction immediately following his narrow victory over the French in the Battle of Lake George. Shortly before this battle, he had renamed the lake in honor of King George. The French and British had been struggling for over a century for control of the North American continent. Johnson expected the French to make a major advance down from Canada, invading the colonies along the Lake Champlain–Hudson River route.

For two years, the fort was used as a staging area for English raiding parties. It was from here that Major Rogers (of Rogers's Rangers fame) launched his daring sorties deep within the French territories.

The French were also busy making probes against the fort; the Marquis de Montcalm, commander of the French forces during the French and Indian War, attacked with a massive force of 10,000 French and Indians. The brave English regulars and Colonial forces under Colonel Monro withstood six days and nights of brutal pounding by French artillery against their garrison. The sounds of battle permeated the air along with shattering logs, gunsmoke, and the scent of blood. With the fort near collapse, Colonel Monro surrendered what was left of his 2,200-man command, along with the women and children in the fort.

Part of the terms of surrender included safe passage for the survivors. But the Algonquin Indians in Montcalm's force were part of a tribe who lived mostly in Canada and parts of northeastern New York and had allied themselves with the French at the beginning of the Colonial period and, consequently, had suffered at the hands of the British and Colonials.

The defenders and their wives and children were sent toward safety under an Indian and French escort, but Montcalm lost control of his Indian allies. They attacked the survivors with a vengeance, decapitating, scalping, and setting them on fire. It was one of the worst massacres in Colonial history. Montcalm set the fort aflame, burning it to the ground, and ordered it covered with sand. It remained that way until 1953 when the restoration project began. Today, the fort is a living museum, and as I entered it I felt as if I were walking into history.

Fort William Henry, a two-story log structure with cannons aimed in all directions, was rebuilt completely to its original specifications. During the summer months, employees in period dress give demonstrations of life as it was at the fort in 1755, complete with cannons and muskets firing and soldiers performing drills. I wandered through the fort, admiring its many displays. Most impressive was a Colonial flintlock rifle found in the lake in 1963; an X-ray of the rifle showed it still had a charge in the barrel. There are numerous arrowheads, guns, uniforms, and other artifacts to see.

I walked down to the dungeon area where prisoners were once chained to the walls or locked in cells no larger than a modern phone booth. From there I went to view the soldiers' graveyard, just outside the fortress walls.

Robert Rogers was an American frontiersman who fought under the British during the French and Indian Wars (1754–1763) and led a group of raiders called Rogers's Rangers. His daring exploits made him a Colonial hero. However, during the Revolution he wasn't trusted by either side, having fought for both. Rogers was captured by the Continentals and held by General Washington as a spy. He escaped to England in 1780 where he died in poverty in 1795.

Where Armies Trod.
Fort William Henry in Lake George Village, constructed in 1755, was once a staging area for English raids against the French.

I recalled seeing this area many years ago with the morbid curiosity of a child, but now the effect was entirely different. I felt it was almost sacrilegious to gaze at the skeletal remains of soldiers who perished over 200 years ago.

Archaeologists had discovered these remains during the restoration. Some had crushed skulls, and it is believed this was done during the massacre. Other soldiers still had their uniforms' cuff links attached to the bones of their wrists by rust. As I walked back to the docks, I couldn't help but wonder if we should not have allowed these soldiers to rest in peace and once again cover them with the earth they fought so valiantly to defend.

On the Lake

Three cruise ships take visitors for rides on Lake George. The *Ticonderoga*, the largest, is 167 feet long and can carry 500 passengers. Built in 1944, it was originally a troop carrier in World War II. The *Minne-Ha-Ha*, built in 1969, is an actual replica of a steam-wheeled paddleboat modeled after the famous Mississippi River steamboats. One hundred and three feet

Wheels across the Water.
The *Mohican*, a 115-foot-long steam-powered paddle wheeler, was built in 1908. Today, along with her sister ships, *Ticonderoga* and *Minne-Ha-Ha*, she carries thousands of sightseers across the deep, silent waters of Lake George each year.

long, it can carry 400 passengers. Both these boats take short cruises on the lake. The *Mohican,* built in 1908, also has a capacity of 400, is 115 feet long and cruises the entire length of the lake (about a five-hour round trip). Some of the ships offer dinner cruises and Dixieland jazz. For reservations and up-to-date information, call the Lake George Steamship Company, which has been carrying passengers since 1817, at (518) 668-5777.

If you're touring with children, Lake George Village has several attractions they'll love. Gaslight Village, located near the fort and dock, has an 1890s atmosphere, forty rides, an ice revue, and a car museum. Magic Forest, located on State Route (SR) 9, is a multi-theme fun park with Santa, live shows, and rides. I hated to leave the village, but as the day progressed it became more crowded, so I headed north on SR 9N.

The Lake George Scenic Drive

Much of the scenery from Lake George Village to Bolton Landing has been marred by overdevelopment, but from that point on, the shoreline retains its rustic charm. I stopped briefly in Bolton Landing to view two interesting sites.

The Church of Saint Sacrament, a beautiful old stone building with stained-glass windows, was constructed in 1869. The church's name is derived from the original name of Lake George, Lac du Saint Sacrament, or Lake of the Blessed Sacrament.

Overlooking Lake George, the massive resort complex, The Sagamore, occupies its own seventy-acre island and is listed on the National Register

Sanctuary of Stone.
The lovely Church of Saint Sacrament is one of the highlights of a visit to Bolton Landing.

Luxury on the Lake.
Originally opened in 1883, the famous Sagamore Resort is one of the most elegant hotels in New York state. Located on Green Island in Lake George, the hotel is a classic example of nineteenth-century charm and grandeur.

of Historic Buildings. Originally opened in 1883, its spacious and luxurious accommodations soon became a mecca for a very select international clientele. In 1981, a Philadelphia entrepreneur, Norman Wolgin, purchased the hotel and decided to restore it to its former grandeur. More than $72,000,000 have been spent on the restoration, and today The Sagamore stands as a classic of nineteenth-century charm and a perfect example of the luxurious hotels of the 1880s.

The Sagamore has 350 rooms and suites, as well as several beautiful dining rooms overlooking the lake. Other amenities include an 18-hole, 188-acre championship golf course, 2 indoor and 4 lighted all-weather tennis courts, an indoor/outdoor pool, and a large wooden yacht that serves as a floating restaurant in the warm-weather season.

Of course, most of the facilities are for guests only, but the restaurants are open to the public and offer a nice way to enjoy the beauty of The Sagamore. The white hotel itself is of classical design, with numerous tall columns and porches. Its majestic setting on Green Island is not a sight easily forgotten. I was impressed enough to want to return in the future as a guest.

Backyard Beauty.
The Sagamore's manicured grounds are but a small part of the hotel's offerings. Other amenities include an eighteen-hole golf course, indoor tennis courts, swimming pool, and even a floating restaurant.

Just north of Bolton Landing is a fantastic overlook of the lake, with mountains rising steeply from the shore. At this point the road becomes challenging as it winds its way up Tongue Mountain. The road is well paved but full of curves, hills, and a few steep ascents and descents; it is not prohibitive of big rigs. There are several excellent trails in the Tongue Mountain area; you can hike the entire Tongue Mountain Range, making a circular trip in roughly eight hours, covering 12.4 miles. This trail takes you over several mountains that offer expansive views of the lake and along the shoreline. You can also hike small sections of the trail and then return the same way.

The last plunging slope of Tongue Mountain kept me concentrating on my steering. At the bottom, I pulled off onto the Tongue Mountain overlook to relax with one of the prettiest views in New York. The overlook sits on a cliff, high above the lake, offering wide views of Lake George, with the contrast of steep mountains against whitecapped waves glittering in the sunlight.

Refreshed, I continued on SR 9N toward Hague, a small beach town with several quaint old buildings.

Pinnacle of Lake George Charm

I drove along SR 9N through Hague, appreciating its fine views, and then turned into Rogers' Rock Public Campground. Although there are many campgrounds in the area (check your *Trailer Life Campground & RV Services Directory* for a complete listing), Rogers' Rock is my favorite.

One of the main attractions is the lake itself, which offers a diversity of water sports including swimming, skiing, skin diving, fishing, boating, and canoeing. (There's a launching and docking area at the campground.) Lake George covers 28,200 acres, with a maximum width of 3 miles and depths up to 200 feet. The lake is a fisherman's paradise with lake, brown, and rainbow trout, salmon, bass, northern pike, and yellow perch. Boats, canoes, and sailboats can be rented in Hague and Ticonderoga.

Since large sections of the lake border wilderness, there is ample wildlife in the region, including deer, bobcat, beaver, otter, mink, raccoon, and black bear. On previous visits I have seen a bobcat and a weasel, but I didn't spot any this trip, with the exception of the raccoons that had a field day knocking over the garbage can.

After I set up camp, I headed for the lake, only fifty yards from my site. As usual, the water was invigorating. I floated on the small waves of the inlet and gazed toward the beach and Rogers' Rock Mountain rising behind it. The mountain is an impressive sight since it appears to be one solid piece of rock (it isn't) rising straight up hundreds of feet from the water's edge to the top.

Legend has it that when Major Rogers was being pursued by Indians, he escaped capture by sliding down the rock face of the mountain to the freedom and safety of Lake George below. The Indians didn't follow. Having observed the slide from both the top of the mountain looking down and from a boat in the water looking up, I could see why.

A trail to the top of the mountain begins behind campsite No. 181. It takes a little over two hours round-trip and is relatively easy. On a clear day the view is awesome, with far-reaching panoramas of the lake, mountains, and Vermont. You can also continue all the way to the slide and see the spot where Rogers eluded the Indians. This popular hike is easy enough for the entire family.

The Stuff from Which Canoes Were Made.
White-barked mountain birch trees are one of many species of trees that blanket the rugged mountains surrounding Lake George.

On the Freedom Trail

The drive from the camp to "Ti" (population 8,374), as the town of Ticonderoga is called, is a scenic one, with views of farmland and mountains. Ti, one of the first lumber towns in the Adirondacks, was created from the old town of Crown Point on March 20, 1804. The earliest settlers to the area came mostly from Vermont and wrote about wolves howling in the night and massive black bears wandering through the forest. The town

View from Tongue Mountain.
Photographers shouldn't miss the scenic views of Lake George from the Tongue Mountain Road near Bolton Landing.

Lake Overview.
Near Rogers' Rock Campground, this highway pullout offers travelers a grand view of Lake George.

developed around the mills along the LaChute River, which runs through the town center from Lake George and drains into Lake Champlain.

Ticonderoga developed into a classic company town, deriving much of its income and employment from the International Paper Company's plant. At one time, visitors avoided the town because the paper mill sat at its center, spewing its odoriferous fumes. Thankfully for both residents and visitors alike, the plant was torn down and relocated outside of town.

Mount Defiance.
Visitors will be rewarded with wide-reaching views of Lake Champlain and Lake Champlain Valley from atop Mount Defiance.

My first stop here was to visit the two impressive falls of the LaChute River. Unfortunately, the falls had been destroyed in order to harness their hydroelectric power. A battle was waged in this tiny town for many months over whether to use the falls to generate power or leave them for their beauty. Sadly, I think, power won and we all lost. Upset over the demise of the falls, I followed the town signs to Mount Defiance.

Top of the World

The road up Mount Defiance is somewhat steep and narrow, with a few tight curves. My small motorhome didn't have any difficulties, but larger ones might. The view is spectacular: I could see a large portion of the Champlain Valley running along the New York–Vermont border between the Adirondack Mountains and the Green Mountains. Below was the lower end of Lake Champlain and sitting on the shore of the lake, the impressive stone fortress, Fort Ticonderoga. From this vantage point I could see how British General John Burgoyne, with his artillery trained on the fort, was able to force the Americans to surrender without firing a shot.

A Side Trip to Pharaoh Lakes Wilderness

The Pharaoh Lakes Wilderness contains thirty-six bodies of water within its 46,039 acres of land. It can be reached by taking SR 74 west from Ticonderoga, turning left onto Putnam Pond Road, and following it to Putnam Pond Public Campground. The drive from the town and into the campground offers some beautiful mountain views. The rustic campground welcomes travelers with large wooded sites, a pond for swimming, fishing, and boating, and trailheads into the wilderness.

Forty-eight miles of trails allow for a wide range of hiking ability. If you like a challenge, it's possible to take a fifteen-mile day hike on trails that pass sixteen wilderness lakes and ponds. Of course, I don't recommend it unless you're in excellent shape. However, there are many short, easy trails into the wilderness, allowing you to experience its beauty at your own pace.

One of the best hikes is to the Pharaoh Mountain fire tower. From its 2,556-foot summit, the view encompasses the entire wilderness area, offering spectacular scenes of mountains, lakes, ponds, and jagged cliffs. The trail is not difficult for the experienced hiker but does require about half a day to complete.

Fishing opportunities are superb; fishermen have told me that the fish are delicious because of "being nurtured in the crystal waters of the wilderness lakes and ponds." Numerous short hikes lead to lovely locations that provide great spots for fishing and picnicking.

Fort Ticonderoga

I continued on SR 9N through Ticonderoga, following the signs to the fort. There are many historic markers along the way identifying troop placement and events. Between 1755 and 1777, Fort Ticonderoga was attacked six times; three times it surrendered and three times the invaders were repulsed. The flags of three nations flew over it: France, England, and America. The building itself is a massive stone structure, its high walls lined with cannons, with a commanding view of Lake Champlain and the surrounding countryside. The sounds of a fife and drum corps drifted over the fortress walls as I entered. Later there would be a demonstration of the loading, aiming, and firing of the cannon.

The French began construction in 1755 and named it Fort Carillon. The fort controlled access to Lake Champlain and Lake George and was referred to as the "Key to the Continent."

In 1758 the French successfully defended Fort Carillon against an attack by 15,000 British troops, but in 1759 British General Amherst captured and rebuilt the fort, and it acquired its present name.

Ethan Allen and his Green Mountain Boys took the fort for America in a bloodless surprise attack in 1775; the next year Benedict Arnold assembled the first American fleet here. The fort changed hands again in 1777, when Burgoyne captured it for the British. Later that year the British abandoned the fort and burned all buildings on both sides of the lake. The fort was never garrisoned again.

Parading the Past.
Volunteers dressed in eighteenth-century army uniforms wander the grounds of Fort Ticonderoga during visiting hours, answering questions from tourists and presenting demonstrations on the use of Early American weapons. The massive fort was built in 1755 by the French.

Tour Guides.
Snappily dressed tour guides at Fort Ticonderoga stand beside an ancient cannon.

After the Revolutionary War, Columbia University acquired title, which it held until 1820. William Pell, a wealthy merchant, bought it from Columbia and began restoration; it was opened to the public in 1909. Fort Ticonderoga is still owned and operated by the Pell family, namely John H. G. Pell, the great great grandson of William Pell.

While listening to the music of the fife and drums, I looked over the museum's large collection of maps, powder horns, etchings, rifles, and paintings on display. Many of the articles were found around the fort; in fact, the museum has more articles actually used by Colonial and Revolutionary soldiers than any other museum in the United States.

I walked atop the stone walls, gazing over the farmland and forest that surround the fort. Across the waters of Lake Champlain, I could see the flag flying over Mount Defiance.

Historic Crown Point

Leaving the fort, I continued north on SR 9N/22, traveling through the rural Champlain Valley with its many farms, country villages, and views of the Adirondacks looming far off on the western horizon. The rest of the tour took me through the valley and along parts of Lake Champlain's shoreline. The distinctive old buildings and Colonial homes of Crown Point (population, 1,800) drew me in.

An interesting section of Crown Point is the Ironville National Historic District, which, as its name attests, was once an ironworks area. I made a right onto Ironville Road and traveled seven miles to the hamlet and the

Ancient Ironville.
The Penfield Museum in the Ironville National Historic District is filled with memorabilia and artifacts from the nineteenth century. Industrial electricity was first used here in the early 1800s.

Penfield Museum. The museum is housed in the Penfield Mansion, a large, white clapboard Colonial home with a front porch and a country-style white wood fence encircling it. The museum grounds cover 500 acres, and the mansion is filled with memorabilia of the nineteenth-century iron-works community: paintings, original furnishings, exhibits on the iron-ore industry, and Civil War artifacts from Crown Point.

Electricity for industrial purposes was used for the first time at Allen Penfield's ironworks. He introduced the use of a large electromagnet that eventually served as a stepping stone toward the invention of the electric motor.

I returned to SR 9N/22 by the same route, continuing north for several miles to the Crown Point State Historic Site.

Remnants of History

At Crown Point Historical Site I found the carefully preserved ruins of Fort St. Frederick, which had been a major French stronghold in the Champlain Valley. It had helped secure the French claim to this region from 1737 to 1759, when it fell to the British during the French and Indian War. In the same general location, the British built Fort Crown Point, which was captured by the Americans in 1775. There are historical and archaeological exhibits at the visitor center. Unfortunately, it was closed the day I was there (open Wednesday through Sunday). Nevertheless, I enjoyed seeing the roofless stone barracks, walking across stone-reinforced dirt walls, and reading the historical markers. I could see Lake Champlain and the Champlain Bridge crossing over to Vermont. Although the ruins can't possibly be compared with Fort Ticonderoga and Fort William Henry, they have a charm all their own. The quiet solitude of their rural setting and the stark remnants of their once-great existence create a unique aura.

I returned to SR 9N/22 from the Crown Point access road and continued north to pass through Port Henry, which claims to have its own Loch Ness-style monster, the "Champ." According to local folklore, the Champ is a serpentlike prehistoric beast that has made Bulwagga Bay, famous for its superior fishing, its home. A sign on SR 9N/22 lists the names and dates of people who have sighted the Champ. Some of the dates extend back to the late 1800s. A few miles north of Port Henry, SR 9N and SR 22 separate; I continued north on SR 22.

Stepping into Small-Town America

Essex is the epitome of small-town charm. This lovely hamlet overlooks Lake Champlain and was listed in its entirety on the National Register of Historic Places in 1975. Founded in 1765 by Irish colonial William Gilliland, Essex prospered until the Revolution, when it was completely destroyed. But because of its prime location in the resource-rich northern frontier, it rapidly rose from the ashes and became prosperous again. By the middle of the 1800s, it was one of the busiest towns on the lake, with a population of over 2,000. But as the frontier moved west, Essex fell into decline. By

Common Sight.
Red barns are as common in New York farm country as are cacti in the deserts of Arizona. This one is located near the historic town of Essex.

the late 1860s, its population had dwindled to 1,600, and the residents were forced to make do with what they had; the hamlet has changed little since then.

A walking tour seemed just the thing: I stopped at several stores to look at the antiques, crafts, and artwork, but the buildings are the real attraction. The architectural styles range from Federal and Greek Revival to Colonial. The craftsmanship is impressive even to the untrained eye. Some of the buildings date back to the late 1700s; Wright's Inn, a Federal-style structure built in 1790, is Essex's earliest surviving tavern. The Essex Inn, which is still in business, was built in 1810 in Federal style; in 1835 a Greek Revival colonnade was added.

At the Old Dock Restaurant, which overlooks the lake, the inside dining room has a country feel with thick wood beams and dark wood walls. I chose to eat outside, next to the dock and on the water's edge. As I watched the ferry slowly make its way across Lake Champlain to Vermont and back, I wished I could stay longer in Essex, but I also wanted to reach Ausable Chasm before it closed.

Awesome Ausable

I pushed north on SR 22 and continued to take in the beautiful countryside of the Champlain Valley until I arrived at Ausable. Ausable Chasm, a miniature Grand Canyon that can be viewed on foot or by boat, has been thrilling travelers since 1870. This deep gorge, cut through the rock by the Ausable River, is 1½ miles long, with several waterfalls and sets of rapids. In some places the ancient rock walls rise 100 to 200 feet above the river and are as close as 20 feet apart.

The first explorers of the chasm had to lower themselves into the gorge by ropes extended from the top of the cliff walls. Today, you simply walk down steps, proceeding along stone galleries (rock formations of different shapes and sizes), and cross back and forth over the gorge on steel bridges. I had a great time studying the rock sculptures and creating images from their formations. I particularly enjoyed the boat ride through the narrow, perpendicular walls of the gorge, and riding the rapids. Being in the bottom of the gorge feels as if you have entered the center of the earth. It only takes a few hours to explore the chasm and is well worth the time.

Awesome Ausable.
Two hundred feet deep in places and more than a mile in length, Ausable Chasm in the Champlain Valley is one of the most dramatic sights in the east. The trail into the gorge is steep and difficult in places, so be sure to wear sturdy shoes.

Champlain Ferry.
Car and passenger ferries are major modes of transportation on Lake Champlain, connecting the shores of both New York and Vermont with each other, as well as with the lake's numerous island communities.

The Mighty Waters of Lake Champlain

Although I'd reached the end of my trip, Lake Champlain still offers many other touring experiences. If you own a boat or are willing to rent one, you could spend several days exploring the lake. It covers over 300,000 acres and is 127 miles long, 12 miles across at its widest. Fishermen will find trout, bass, great northern pike, perch, muskellunge, cisco, and bowfin in its waters. There are swimming and camping areas along the shore. Sailboating is especially popular, with strong breezes to fill the sails and miles of scenery to take in while being propelled by the currents of the wind.

You can cruise on Lake Champlain from a point twenty-four miles south of Ticonderoga all the way into Canada. The lake's shoreline encompasses some of the most scenic views in the northeast—forests, mountains, country villages, and farmland. There are also several ferry crossings at various spots along the shore that allow you to cross over into Vermont or simply enjoy the ride back and forth.

As I pulled away from the Ausable Chasm and Lake Champlain, I was aware that my tour had come to a close. But I felt little sadness, for I planned to return to Rogers' Rock for a few days of relaxing on the beach and hiking the trails. And from there, I'd be off on a new adventure in the scenic wilderness of the great Northern Kingdom.

POINTS OF INTEREST: New York Tour 1

Lake George-Champlain Historic Trail

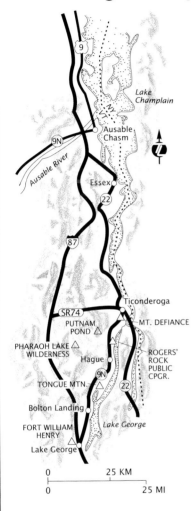

0   25 KM

0   25 MI

ACCESS: *New York Thruway (90)* north to Albany then the *Northway (87)* to Lake George Village exit, north on *SR 9N.*

INFORMATION: *Adirondack Information Center,* I-87 North between exits 17 & 18, Glen Falls (518) 873-6301; *Warren County Tourism,* 801 Municipal Center, Lake George, 12845 (518) 761-6366.

ANNUAL EVENTS:

Lake George Village: *Merchants Sidewalk Bazaar,* June; *Family Fes-* *tival, Arts and Crafts Show, Antique and Classic Boat Rendezvous,* August; *Jazz Festival,* September; *Fall Foliage Festival,* October; *Winter Carnival,* February.

Bolton Landing: *Arts and Crafts Show, Quality Antique Show,* July; *Arts and Crafts Show,* August.

Hague: *Winter Carnival,* February.

Ticonderoga: *Best Fourth in the North Celebration, Scottish Gathering,* July; *Arts Trek Children's Series, Summer Concert Series,* July and August.

Crown Point: *Country Jamboree,* July; *Auctions* and *Flea Markets,* July and August; *Heritage Day at Penfield Museum,* August; *Italian Festival, Fort to Fort 30K Race,* October; *National Ice Auger Championship,* February.

MUSEUMS AND GALLERIES:

Lake George: *Fort William Henry,* Beach Road (518) 668-5471, restored fort, historic items, artifacts, and paintings, open daily May 1–mid-October, 9 A.M.–5 P.M.; *Lake George Historic Association,* Canada/Amherst Street (518) 688-5044, daily 10 A.M.–5 P.M., July–August, September–June by appointment; *Adirondack Adventure* (518) 688-9615, same address as above, multi-image slide show of Adirondacks, daily Memorial–Columbus days.

Bolton Landing: *Historical Society Museum,* Lakeshore Drive (518) 644-9060, late June–September, Tuesday, Thursday, and Saturday, call for hours.

Ticonderoga: *Hancock House, Moses Circle Museum* and reproduction of original John Hancock house in Boston (518) 585-7868, July–August, daily 10 A.M.–4 P.M., September–June, Wednesday–Saturday 10 A.M.–4 P.M.; *Fort Ticonderoga,* SR 74 (518) 585-2821, restored fort, museum, and gallery, daily mid-May–mid-October, 9 A.M.–5 P.M.

Crown Point: *Penfield Homestead Museum and Historical Recreation Area,* Ironville Rd. (518) 597-3804, mid-May–October 15, Tuesday–Sunday 10 A.M.–5 P.M.

SPECIAL ATTRACTIONS:

Lake George: *Parasailing Rides over Lake George* (518) 688-3280; *Gaslight Village Park,* Lake George Village (518) 668-5459, rides, shows, museum, open daily June 20–Labor Day; *The Great Escape Fun Park,* Lake George Village (518) 798-1084, 100 rides, shows, and attractions, open daily Memorial Day–Labor Day, 9:30 A.M.–6 P.M.; *Water Slide World,* Lake George Village (518) 668-4407, wave pool, water slides, toddler lagoon, open daily June 15–Labor Day, 10 A.M.–6:30 P.M.; *Magic Forest,* Lake George Village (518) 668-2448, rides, shows, magic, open daily Memorial Day–Labor Day, 9:30 A.M.–6:30 P.M.

Glens Falls: *Adirondack Balloon Flights,* Glens Falls (518) 793-6342, May–October.

OUTFITTERS:

Adirondack Range Guide and Outfitter, Box 8, Hoffmeister, 13353 (315) 826-7416.

Adirondack-Champlain Guide Service, RR 297, Long Pond Lodge, Willsboro, 12996 (518) 963-7351.

RESTAURANTS:

Lake George: *Shoreline Restaurant,* (518) 688-2875; Cajun and Creole cuisine; *Mario's Restaurant* (518) 688-2665; Italian cuisine.

Bolton Landing: *The Sagamore Dining Room,* (518) 644-9400; continental cuisine.

Hague: *Indian Kettles,* (518) 543-6576; seafood.

Ticonderoga: *Wagon Wheel Restaurant,* (518) 585-9700; American.

THE NORTHERN KINGDOM
Heart of the Adirondacks

For thousands the most important passion of life is the overpowering desire to escape periodically from the strangling clutch of mechanistic civilization. To us the enjoyment of solitude, complete independence, and the beauty of undefiled panoramas is absolutely essential to happiness.

Robert Marshall

The Northway is a 175-mile-long highway that runs from Albany to the Canadian border; approximately 105 miles lie along the eastern section of Adirondack State Park. Completed in the early 1960s, the road was constructed to give easy access to the area. Eighty-four miles, from exits 22 to 34, were designated America's most scenic highway for the years 1966–67. I was traveling 50 miles of that section to exit 30.

Albany

Tour **2** *229 miles*

THE NORTHWAY SCENIC DRIVE • KEENE VALLEY • KEENE • HIGH PEAKS WILDERNESS • ADIRONDACK MOUNTAIN CLUB LODGES • ALGONQUIN MOUNTAIN • LAKE PLACID • SARANAC LAKE • ST. REGIS CANOE AREA • PAUL SMITH'S • SIX NATIONS INDIAN MUSEUM • WHITEFACE MOUNTAIN • JAY

Highway to the Adirondacks

As I rolled along the Northway, I saw the vast, mountainous wilderness beckoning me to this north-central region of Adirondack State Park. I felt a growing sense of anticipation as I motored deeper into this immense park. Whether you begin the tour, as I did, just north of Lake George Village, or connect from the previous tour via SR 9N heading southwest from Ausable Chasm, you will find the Northway a most enjoyable ride, with numerous vistas and easy motoring.

It was a clear day, and I could see for miles each time my rig crested another hill. Mountains and forests surrounded me; Schroon Lake glistened at the foot of Pharoah Lakes Wilderness (see page 12). The mountain ranges of my destination rose in the northwest.

Into the Northern Kingdom

I exited and drove north on SR 73 into the heart of the Northern Kingdom—355,000 acres of rugged wilderness, hundreds of ponds and lakes, miles of trails and scenic roads, and the highest mountains in New York. It's a region offering many opportunities to experience nature firsthand.

Continuing northwest toward Keene Valley, the road wanders through the 72,000-acre Giant and Dix Mountain Wilderness areas. There are numerous trailheads along SR 73 that lead into over forty-eight miles of trails. The serpentine road makes for some slow driving but presents no other problems.

On both sides of the road, massive cliffs block out part of the sky. Pine trees wall the road and small lakes dot the foot of the mountains. I stopped at Chapel Pond, where SR 73 runs through the middle of a deep, dark gorge and huge cliffs rise from the water's edge, to watch a few fishermen and canoeists drift across a pond. This area is popular with rock climbers but was off limits temporarily because of the possible danger to several nests of peregrine falcons. The falcons are a federally protected endangered species. They were once common throughout the Adirondacks, but due to the adverse effects of the insecticide DDT not a single nesting pair remained by the 1950s. In 1974 a program was instituted to reintroduce

Chapel Pond.
Adjacent to State Road 73, the quiet beauty of Chapel Pond is inviting to picnickers, anglers, and canoeists.

Casting for Trout.
On the Ausable River, an angler carefully presents a tiny artificial fly to feeding rainbow trout.

them to the area, a program that continues successfully today. Unable to spot any of the rare raptors as I scanned the sky, I decided to drive on.

Beyond Chapel Pond, SR 73 shoots down a steep hill and offers a great view of the High Peaks Wilderness rising in the distance. The town of Keene Valley sits on the edge of the High Peaks Wilderness and is a popular area, although it wasn't always so. During the American Revolution, New York offered free land as an inducement for soldiers willing to defend the northern borders. At the end of the war, no one claimed the land, and it reverted back to the state.

The Adirondack Mountain Club Area

Times have certainly changed, and today Keene Valley is a hikers' and backpackers' paradise. The Adirondack Mountain Club (ADK) is a nonprofit organization founded in 1922 to preserve and protect New York's Catskill and Adirondack parks. The club maintains two lodges in the High Peaks and sponsors workshops, seminars, and educational programs.

If you don't want to backpack, the club's Johns Brook Lodge in the hamlet of Keene Valley offers the opportunity to experience the wilderness from a comfortable base. You can hike 3½ miles to the lodge and enjoy a bed, breakfast, and dinner there while exploring the trails during the day. Reservations are required before hiking to the lodge, and they should be made well in advance of any planned stay.

While in Keene Valley, I stopped at The Mountaineer, a complete outdoor supply store. They have an extensive map selection for the Adirondacks, as well as a number of books on the area. If you like to hike, backpack, fish, or canoe, don't pass it by. A blackboard outside the entrance displays the daily weather report and the backcountry bug situation. After looking over the items in The Mountaineer, I continued motoring north toward Keene, surrounded by more pleasant views of the valley and the mountains.

Stopping to buy gas in Keene, I was impressed by this small, quaint town. There are two small restaurants; the one with a western motif and front-porch dining especially appealed to me. But Keene's major attraction is the North Country Taxidermy. I'm not a hunter myself, but I was fascinated by the realistic displays of bear, deer, coyote, bobcat, beaver, and raccoon, all native to the region. The store also sells fur hats, moccasins, and jewelry.

Remember When?
The gasoline price on this ancient pump at an antique store in Upper Jay reads 36¢ per gallon.

The High Peaks Wilderness

The High Peaks, the largest wilderness area in the Adirondacks, is famous well beyond the borders of New York State for its rugged beauty. The 226,435-acre region contains 112 bodies of water, 238 miles of foot trails, and 58 miles of horse trails.

At the turnoff for the Adirondack Lodge, I could see the gigantic peaks rising from the field; they reminded me of the Tetons in Jackson Plain,

Heading High.
An RVer heads for the High Peaks Wilderness near Lake Placid.

Wyoming. Many westerners scoff at the comparably low heights of the eastern mountains, but they forget that the base of an eastern mountain is only a few hundred feet above sea level while the base of a western mountain is several thousand feet above sea level. The difference is really one of perception.

The Adirondack Mountain Club Lodge is the access point for the trails leading into the interior of the High Peaks area. The complex has a parking lot, a lodge, an information center, and a small, rustic campground used by many RVers and tent campers as a base for hiking trips. The ADK owns part of the land in this area and, along with the state, helps maintain the trails. They supply trail information, and a ranger is usually on duty to answer questions. Even if you don't care to hike, it's worth the drive in, and the road is good enough for large motorhomes. The trails are very popular because this region, as its name denotes, has the highest mountains in New York.

After setting up camp, I pulled out my maps to find a good route for a short hike. Tom Mullee, a camper from Staten Island, saw me studying the maps and introduced himself. He suggested climbing Mount Jo. "It's less than two miles round-trip and easy enough for a novice hiker. The view is great."

Tom was right. I returned to camp in less than four hours and had an unhurried time enjoying the view of the peaks and Heart Lake from the summit. Another very easy hike of similar length is to Marcy Lake. The lake's beauty makes it one of the most popular short hikes.

A Climb up Algonquin Mountain

Algonquin Mountain takes its name from the Indians who lived here. The Iroquois called them Ha-De-Ron-Dah *or "bark-eaters" because they ate tree bark. The name* Adirondack *is also derived from this Indian name.*

I was up early the next day and decided to climb Algonquin Mountain, the second-highest peak in New York State at 5,114 feet. Although Mount Marcy is the highest at 5,344 feet, I didn't climb it for several reasons. First of all, the trail is considerably longer; secondly, Art Rippas, a friend who hikes extensively in the area, said the view from Algonquin is better; and thirdly, since Mount Marcy is the highest, it attracts the most hikers, leaving Algonquin less traveled.

Years ago I had climbed it with my wife, Linda, and was excited about doing it again. The last time up, Linda left me in the dust and beat me to the summit. This time she wasn't along to show me up. The trail is tough, about eight miles round-trip, and I felt every bit of it. Parts of the trail are seriously eroded, and I had to jump from rock to rock. I struggled along, forcing myself upward toward the rocky summit. When I broke out above the treeline, I could see part of the peak slicing across the sky.

Finally I reached the last major ascent, a climb of 912 feet but less than a mile in distance. I clambered up the rocky trail until I stood on the alpine summit in triumph. The 360-degree view is spectacular; I felt as if I could reach out and touch the clouds as they floated by. It really made the struggle worthwhile. The steep, dark mountains seemed like an unassailable stone fortress forbidding entry into the wilderness. I gazed toward

Where Skiers Soared.
Constructed in 1980, Lake Placid's twenty-six-story Olympic Jumping Complex is an engineering marvel. Visitors can ride to the top in a glass-enclosed elevator.

Lake Placid and picked out the 1980 Olympic Tower, a monument to civilization's engineering genius. Walking around the pine-scented summit, I marveled at the expansive view.

If you'd like to try the trip up Algonquin Mountain, don't let the difficulty of the hike discourage you; I saw hikers of all ages on the summit. The key is to hike slowly and allow for plenty of time. The ranger at the lodge can answer any questions before you go. Be prepared for weather changes; temperatures can be considerably colder on top. One ranger told me they can get snow twelve months a year, and hikers should be prepared for it.

The mountain was named in 1880 by Verplank Colvin, lawyer, topographical engineer, and the person most responsible for the Adirondack survey, which resulted in the great forest preserve of this region. He was one of our first conservationists. The name was chosen to honor the vanquished Algonquin Indian tribes that had ruled this region until their alliance with the French against the British proved to be with the "wrong" side. Their power and dominance over the region was lost forever.

On the Glory Road to Lake Placid

Lake Placid (population 2,800) has twice hosted the Winter Olympics (in 1932 and 1980). A self-guided tour of the facilities with the help of a map and brochure begins a few miles beyond the Adirondack Lodge on SR 73 at the Olympic Sports Complex.

The Olympic Sports Complex at Mount Van Hoevenberg is the site of the bobsled and luge runs. A trolley car can take you to the start of the run, one mile up Mount Van Hoevenberg, and you can walk through the complex for a closer look. It's interesting to see the films of the competitions and the many historic photographs.

The next stop on the tour is the Olympic Jumping Complex. A ride to the top of the ski jump in a glass-enclosed elevator climbs twenty-six stories and provides far-reaching views of Lake Placid and the surrounding countryside. The ski jump is 600 feet from the foot of the lower hill to the top of tower. The ski jumps are equipped with plastic matting that creates snowlike conditions when wet. This allows for the exciting opportunity to watch the jumpers who now train and compete year-round.

The highlight of the Olympic Tour is Whiteface Mountain, but I planned on visiting it later in my tour, so instead I drove to a historic farm and grave site.

"John Brown's Body Lies Amoulderin' in the Grave"

Just beyond the ski jump is the John Brown Farm Historic Site. This impassioned abolitionist moved his family to the Adirondacks in 1849 to help a small, struggling community of black farmers (derisively dubbed "Timbuctoo" by white settlers who resented their presence). The venture

John Brown's Body.
A favorite visitor stop near Lake Placid is the John Brown Farm Historic Site. The infamous abolitionist, hanged for treason just before the Civil War, is buried here.

failed because the land was not suited for cultivation, and the black farmers, like many Adirondack settlers, were unable to adapt to the rigors of the winters. But this place remained home to Brown, and he returned here between his excursions for liberation.

Brown believed he was an agent of God, a nemesis whose purpose was to bring down the wrath of justice on slaveholders. It was with this belief that he hatched a plan to lead slaves down the path of glory in a bloody revolt against Southern slaveholders. As Brown himself once prophetically remarked, "I am not incapable of error and I may be wrong, but I think that perhaps my object will be nearer fulfillment if I should die." How right he was: Brown's futile attempt to capture the arsenal at Harper's Ferry cost him his life. His two sons were killed, and he was hanged for treason and murder. His body was buried at his farm in 1859, and within a few years soldiers went marching off to the Civil War singing "John Brown's body lies amoulderin' in the grave" as part of their battle cry for freedom.

Brown's small, weather-beaten clapboard house serves as a museum for the mementos of his life. This simple two-story structure belies the passionate nature of the man. Besides the house, barn, and grave marker, there's also an impressive bronze statue of Brown standing defiantly with his arm around a young black man as if leading him to freedom.

From the farm, I continued on SR 73 into the center of Lake Placid, moving along the Olympic Tour which ends at Whiteface Mountain, my next day's destination. The Olympic Center is worth a stop, even though it's not included in the tour, since it is the largest ice complex of its kind in the world. Four ice surfaces are housed under one roof, all open to the public. The site hosts a variety of entertainment events and is the future location of the Lake Placid Winter Olympic Sports Museum, scheduled for completion sometime in late 1989 or 1990.

Despite a few modern buildings, most of the town retains its country charm. Lake Placid began almost 200 years ago as a farming outpost and later became an ironworks community. During the Victorian Age it was a leading resort for the rich. In 1904, its fame as a winter resort began when the now-defunct Lake Placid Club, a resort catering to the wealthy, introduced some winter sports new to North America. The club's elaborate buildings are up for auction, but can still be viewed; their future is undetermined. No longer a resort only for the wealthy, Lake Placid continues to grow more popular every year.

Curious about Lake Placid's history, I stopped at the North Elba Historical Society Museum at the old train station, built in 1867. The museum displays primitive farm implements, canoes, stuffed animals, iron stoves, and many photographs of famous visitors, old landmarks, and hotels.

Leaving the museum, I wandered around exploring the old buildings, crafts stores, and galleries nearby. The Country Kitchen serves a delicious meal, and the Lake Placid Gallery has a variety of good paintings and crafts on display. Horse-drawn carriages also tour the town, and boats cruise around the lake.

Monument to an Abolitionist.
Adjacent to John Brown's simple two-story farm, this bronze monument pays tribute to the abolitionist's defiant battle against slavery.

Peaceful Saranac.
Well-kept homes like this one dot the quiet shores of Saranac Lake.

The Saranac Lakes Water Kingdom

The Saranac Lakes region is a haven for those who love water sports such as fishing, boating, swimming, and canoeing. In fact, the principal lakes in the Adirondack State Park, of which these are a part, form an almost continuous chain, making possible a 150-mile canoe trip (with short portages) through the park. Over ten lakes and ponds in the Saranac Lakes chain are loaded with bass, northern pike, landlocked salmon, lake, rainbow and brown trout, and yellow perch.

The town of Saranac Lake (population, 5,600) was settled in 1819 and became a major center for tuberculosis patients in the late 1800s. In fact, the entire Adirondacks were said to have had health-restoring powers, and many of the early visitors came for that purpose. I can't verify the validity of the claims, but I know I always feel better after a few days here.

The town has several old buildings with second-floor balconies and wooden facades that are reminiscent of structures in the Old West. Robert Louis Stevenson's residence, the Stevenson Memorial Cottage, maintained by the Stevenson Society of America, is a simple, two-story, white clapboard cottage with a large porch extending around three sides, the yard enclosed by a low, white fence. For six months from 1887 to 1888, Steven-

son lived here under the care of Dr. Edward Trudeau, the New York physician who established the first outdoor sanatorium for tuberculosis patients in Saranac Lake. Here, in the place he referred to as his "Little Switzerland in the Adirondacks," Stevenson wrote a number of essays and finished the *Master of Ballantrae*. Many of the original furnishings are still in the cottage.

Saranac Lake also has a golf course, boat launching sites, canoe routes through the lakes, tennis courts and, in the winter, both downhill and cross-country skiing, and snowmobile trails. A storm front starting to move in from the west convinced me to cancel my planned canoe trip, so I continued on SR 3 along the shore, a lovely drive with lakes and forests on both sides of the road.

There are numerous campgrounds in the Saranac area (check the *Trailer Life Campground & RV Services Directory* for listings). Most of the larger lakes allow motorboats, while the smaller ones permit only canoes and rowboats.

The St. Regis Canoe Area

Turning right onto SR 30 at the junction, I headed north toward Fish Creek Pond and Rollins Pond, two state campgrounds I planned to explore. Sitting high in my motorhome, I was able to catch many views of the lakes as I drove toward the campground. This is a most attractive campsite, encircling the shoreline of the two small lakes. All the sites at Fish Creek are on the water, but they are close together. Most of the sites at Rollins Pond are on the water but afford more privacy. Motoring into Rollins Pond,

I went through dense pine forest that rose high into the sky, the tops almost out of sight.

Because of unpromising weather, I continued driving. Back on SR 30, I spotted several canoeists and a small motorboat coming through the forest down a stream that fed into a lake on the opposite side of the road. I wanted to watch them portage so I stopped and jumped from my rig but, to my surprise, they disappeared. A large pipe ran under the road, and they had simply ducked and sailed through it. I watched them paddle into the damp mist rolling over the lake and was sorry I hadn't rented a canoe at Rollins Pond. The bleak weather added to the sense of solitude and primeval nature that seems to permeate the forest. A cold drizzle nudged me on.

At Paul Smith's College, I turned right onto SR 192. Paul Smith's was originally a hotel established in 1859 by Appolos A. Smith, who preferred being called Paul. He was a guide for wealthy sportsmen and quite notorious in his day for many of his outlandish attitudes. He certainly didn't believe in the adage "the customer is always right." Once, because he didn't like the looks of a new guest, he told him, "Don't bother to unpack, mister. Coach out front leaves in the morning." Another time he forgot to bill a guest for a pair of rubber boots and couldn't remember which guest, so he directed his clerk to bill everybody, figuring no one would notice.

Yet many of the wealthiest Manhattan families visited his lodge year after year; the Harrimans, Reids, and Vanderbilts were regular guests. Smith also disregarded the gaming laws, feeling they interfered with the pleasure of his guests. But as the years passed, he realized his folly and in the 1890s testified in Albany in favor of stricter gaming laws.

Smith died in 1912 and his sons ran the hotel until 1930, when it burned to the ground, never to be rebuilt. When they died, the entire estate and its thousands of acres went to found Paul Smith's College of Forestry and Hotel Management.

Immediately after turning onto SR 192, I discovered the Episcopal Chapel of St. John's of the Wilderness, a beautiful little stone structure tucked away in the woods. Originally built of oiled logs, it was established in 1877, burned in 1928, and rebuilt in 1930. Next to the church is an old country graveyard. I was surprised at the young age at which many of the people died, a testament to the hardships of the times.

Leaving the church, I took CR 31 to CR 30. This is a picturesque route into Onchiota (their sign reads "67 of the friendliest people in the Adirondacks plus a few soreheads"). The only two stores were out of business; the nearest place for supplies was ten miles away, and they didn't even have peanut butter! I camped at Buck Pond Campground, on a large, wooded, private site. Here the pond connects to Lake Kushaqua, where you could canoe for twenty-five miles.

Church of the Wildwood.
Near Paul Smith's College, the lovely Episcopal Chapel of St. John's of the Wilderness was originally erected in 1877.

Rollins Pond.
Canoe enthusiasts enjoy a quiet paddle trip on Rollins Pond, part of the Adirondacks's famous St. Regis Canoe Area.

The Iroquois Confederacy of the Five Nations was formed about 1570 and consisted of the Cayuga, Mohawk, Oneida, Onondaga, and Seneca tribes. They later became a confederacy of six nations with the addition of the Tuscarora tribe. Numbering some 5,500, they lived in palisaded villages; men hunted and women farmed. Women held high status in the society and descent was matrilineal. They lived in distinctive, bark-covered, rectangular structures known as longhouses, *which became the symbol of the Iroquois. The longhouse also represented the total area covered by the confederacy and, akin to their place in the area, the longhouse door on the east was guarded by the Mohawk and the west door was guarded by the Seneca.*

The Six Nations Indian Museum

The next morning, I visited the Six Nations Indian Museum, located a half-mile from Buck Pond east on CR 30. It's a small, family-run museum full of Indian artifacts depicting the history of the Six Nations, also known as the Iroquois Confederacy, a remarkably well-organized group of Indian nations that endured for over two centuries.

Indian legend has it that Mohawk Chief Hiawatha founded the League of Five Nations in 1570 to stop the wars between the different nations. The Five Nations were later joined by the Tuscaroras in 1715 after they were forced from their land by white settlers in the south and had to trek north.

The Six Nations controlled a vast empire extending east from the St. Lawrence River to as far west as Ohio. They have been credited with influencing the development of our democratic ideals and helping to set an example for unification of the colonies. Benjamin Franklin wrote in 1754:

> It would be a strange thing if six nations of ignorant savages should be capable of forming a scheme for such a union and be able to execute it in such a manner as that it has subsisted ages and appears indissoluble; and yet that a like union should be impracticable for ten or a dozen English colonies, to whom it is more necessary and must be advantageous. . . .

I spoke with the proprietor, John David Fadden, a Mohawk Indian born on the St. Regis Indian Reservation. His father started the museum over thirty-five years ago. John, an artist and teacher, described the items on display and told me about the Indian history of the area. It was interesting to view history from the Indian perspective, that of a vanquished people upon whose ashes the new nation was built. After all, their lives, their land, and their nations were destroyed to pay for the rise of the new country. John believes strongly in preserving his heritage, and hopes his son will carry on after him.

I continued on CR 30 until it connected with SR 3, then turned right at the Silver Lake sign onto Alder Brook Road, weaving and bouncing along this backcountry route. It was slow going, but the road can handle all types of RVs. Passing MacIntyer's Union Falls Campground, I caught a glimpse of Whiteface Mountain and the falls spilling over the dam and into the woods. At Hawkeye, I took Silver Lake Road and passed Taylor Pond State Primitive Campground. On the left were rocky cliffs and pine-covered hills; to my right, Whiteface on the horizon.

Up Whiteface Mountain

If you're RVing with children, or just young at heart, you might want to stop at Santa's Workshop at the "north pole," with its fairy-tale houses, activities, rides, and petting zoo, before climbing Whiteface.

Veterans Memorial Highway runs eight miles uphill from Wilmington and terminates 500 feet short of the summit of Whiteface Mountain (4,867 feet), New York's fifth-highest peak. If you're on the Olympic Tour, this is the last stop. There is a trailer-drop-off parking area near the gate; the drive is slow going for big rigs, but the road surface is excellent.

Construction on the highway began in December, 1931, and was completed four years later. Governor Franklin D. Roosevelt threw the first and last shovels of earth. After he became president, he dedicated the highway as a memorial to the soldiers killed in World War II.

The serpentine road up Whiteface provides some spectacular views. Far ahead at the summit sits the castlelike building used for observation. Soon I was above the treeline and felt the chilled alpine air. There were a few hairpin turns and several places where I felt that only a rock wall protected me from plunging into oblivion.

From the parking area, you can either hike to the top or take the elevator that rises through a 500-foot shaft cut through the granite center of the peak. The trail is steep but only a fifth of a mile and very invigorating. The view from the top is astounding, the air fresh and snappy. Unlike other peaks in the Adirondacks, Whiteface is isolated, so on a clear day

Scenic Sunset.
Vistas like this are commonplace near the town of Wilmington.

Reminder of the Past.
This old covered bridge near the town
of Jay was built in 1857 and is still in
use today.

you are able to see almost the entire northern part of the state from the
summit. I had a 360-degree view and could see most of the places I'd been
on my tour: Lake Placid below, Lake Champlain in the distance, and even
the faraway Green Mountains of Vermont.

After an hour or so of walking around on the summit, enjoying the
views from many angles, I drove down the mountain and took SR 86 east
to Jay and its treasure, a covered bridge built in 1857 and still in use. The
bridge was named with the usual Yankee practicality: The Old Covered
Bridge. It doesn't look very sturdy but is (even if you're in a large
motorhome). The longest bridge of its kind in New York, it crosses a lovely
section of the East Branch Ausable River.

Near the bridge are a set of rapids and a placid area in the river. It's a
great place for swimming and enjoying whirlpools. I found my own little
nook and relaxed alongside the friendly residents who were enjoying their
river outings.

While driving south on SR 9N back to Keene, I thought about my tour
and all the sights I had enjoyed. I had climbed several mountains by foot
and wheel; learned about history from the Indian perspective; but best of
all, I had traveled through the vast wilderness, the full grandeur of the
Northern Kingdom.

Heart of the Adirondacks

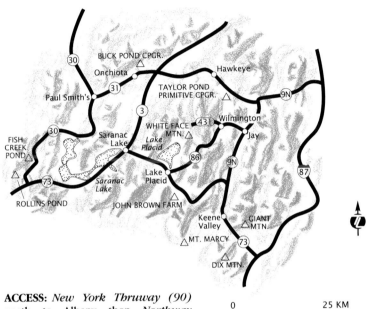

ACCESS: *New York Thruway (90)* north to Albany then *Northway (SR 87)* to exit 30, north on *SR 73.*

INFORMATION: *Department of Commerce Regional Office,* 90 Main Street, Lake Placid, 12946 (518) 523-2412; *Saranac Lake Chamber of Commerce,* 30 Main Street, Saranac Lake 12983 (518) 891-1990; *Adirondack Mountain Club,* 172 Ridge Street, Glens Falls, 12801 (518) 793-7737.

ANNUAL EVENTS:

Lake Placid: *Horse Show, Summer Ice Season, June Bug Festival,* June; *I Love New York Horseshow, Wednesday Evening Sinfonietta Concerts, Outdoor Swim Meet, Ski Jump Competition—70 Meter Hill, Free-Skating Competition, Casio Olympic Tour Triathlon,* July; *Water Skiing Championships,* August; *Quarter Horse Show, Flaming Leaves Square Dance Festival,* September.

Saranac Lake: *Triathlon,* June; *Guideboat/Canoe Race, Park Concerts, Craft Fair, Antique Show and Sale,* July; *Rugby Tournament, Paint and Palette Festival, Firemen's Field Days, Guitar Festival,* August; *90-Mile Canoe Classic,* September; *Alpo Sled Dog Races,* January; *Winter Carnival/Ice Festival,* February.

Wilmington: *Whiteface Mountain 8-mile Uphill Race,* June.

Keene: *Old Mt. Phelps Day, Crafts Fair,* August.

Tupper Lake: *Woodsmen's Days,* July.

MUSEUMS AND GALLERIES:

Lake Placid: *North Elba Historical Society Museum,* Old Train Station, Averyville Road (518) 523-2512, historic items, photographs, memorabilia; June—Sept.; Tuesday—Saturday 1–5 P.M., Friday and Saturday 1–8 P.M., Sunday, 1–5 P.M., closed Monday, admission free; *Lake Placid Center for the Arts,* Saranac Avenue, music, dance, film, theater, workshops, and gallery shows, summer hours Monday—Friday 10 A.M.—5 P.M., weekends 1–5 P.M., gallery free, other prices vary; *Adirondack Store and*

Gallery, Saranac Avenue (518) 523-2646, paintings and prints, fine antiques, twig furniture, and gifts; *The Studio,* 15 Main Street (518) 523-3589, gifts by American artists and craftsmen, art from the North Country.

SPECIAL ATTRACTIONS:

Lake Placid: *Adirondack Flying Service,* Lake Placid (518) 523-2473, scenic flights open year-round, daily 9 A.M.—5 P.M.

Wilmington: *Santa's Workshop,* SR 86 (518) 946-2211, children's rides, crafts, musical shows, open daily Memorial Day—Columbus Day, 9:30 A.M.—4:30 P.M.; *High Falls Gorge,* SR 86 (518) 946-2278, scenic path of waterfalls at base of Whiteface Mountain, gift shop, picnic area, and restaurant, open daily, Memorial weekend—October 10, 8:30 A.M. — 4:30 P.M.

Lake Placid: *Lake Placid Boat Rides,* Holiday Harbor (518) 523-9704, open daily May—October.

OUTFITTERS:

Cold River Ranch, Tupper Lake, 12986 (518) 523-2512.

Middle Earth Expeditions, HCR 01, Lake Placid, 12946 (518) 523-9572.

St. Regis Canoe Outfitters, P.O. Box 318, Lake Clear, 12945 (518) 891-1838.

McDonnell's Adirondack Challenges, P.O. Box 855, Saranac Lake, 12983 (518) 891-1176.

RESTAURANTS:

Lake Clear: *The Lodge* (518) 891-1489; German-American cuisine.

Lake Placid: *Country Kitchen,* Main Street (518) 523-1799; home cooking.

Saranac Lake: *The Red Fox Restaurant,* Route 3 West (518) 891-2127; seafood, steaks, and chops.

The Central Adirondacks

In wildness is the preservation of the world.

Henry David Thoreau

One of the wildest and least-populated areas in Adirondack State Park is the Lakeland Wilderness, lying across its south-central region. A large section of this tour falls within the confines of Hamilton County, with a population under 6,000 and a land area covering 1,735 square miles. This region is rich in natural beauty, history, and wildlife. Bear and deer, which number in the thousands, are very common. The Lakeland Wilderness, once a retreat for both the rich and the unconventional, today remains a major attraction for travelers who enjoy the variety within over 228,000 acres of wilderness. Encompassing hundreds of lakes, ponds, and wild rivers, it gives RVers the unique opportunity to experience the adventure of backwoods wilderness camping without having to backpack. My first stop, the beginning of the tour, was Warrensburg, the last town of any size for many miles.

Tour **3** *172 miles*
Side trip to Stillwater, 36 miles
Side trip to Indian Lake, 69 miles,
one way

WARRENSBURG • NORTH CREEK •
BLUE MOUNTAIN LAKE • RAQUETTE
LAKE • FULTON LAKES • OLD FORGE •
MOOSE RIVER RECREATION AREA

On the Edge of the Wilderness

Warrensburg (population 3,801) is known as the "Antique Capital of the Adirondacks." The twelve antique stores in town are mostly grouped together so customers can easily walk from one to the other. Some stores specialize in particular items, making it easy to locate high-quality antique jewelry, tinware, glass, prints, scientific and musical instruments, clocks, quilts, and Blue Willoware. Every weekend there are townwide "garage sales" that culminate in October with "The Annual World's Largest Garage Sale" on Columbus Day weekend. Over 300 vendors and 100 homes are open for browsing or serious buying.

Once a mill town, Warrensburg sits near the confluence of the Schroon and Hudson rivers, where it derived its energy from dams constructed on the waterways. The mills processed such diverse items as grain, paper, clothing, lumber, and other wood products. Most of the mills are gone, but the town retains a legacy of impressive neoclassical and Victorian homes from that era. I stopped briefly at the Warrensburg Historical Museum at 47 Main Street. Among the many items on display are an 1880s doll carriage, wooden golf clubs, three-wheeled roller skates, and memorabilia from one of Warrensburg's most famous hometown boys, Floyd Bennett (1890–1928), who flew the first aircraft to reach the North Pole. Bennett and Admiral Richard E. Byrd left from Spitsbergen in the Arctic Ocean and flew to the North Pole on May 9, 1926; they received Congressional Medals of Honor for their heroic accomplishments.

Many other activities are available in Warrensburg—canoeing, hiking (up the town's own Hackensack Mountain), golf, horseback riding, swimming, crafts shows, and events featuring live bands for dancing and entertainment. It's best to call the chamber of commerce at (518) 623-2661 for

Lakeshore Living.
Summer homes and cottages dot the shoreline of 6th Lake in the Fulton Chain of Lakes near the resort town of Inlet.

Gardener's Delight.
A roadside flower market in Warrensburg displays a virtual rainbow of living colors.

information about what will be happening during your visit. I left Warrensburg, traveling northwest on SR 28, a scenic mountain drive that allows glimpses of the northern Hudson River.

The Thundering Waters of North Creek

North Creek, a small town of a few hundred people, sits on the edge of the Siamese Ponds Wilderness Area (108,503 acres). Its history began when rugged New Englanders who'd left their farms and villages came to log the region. They fell in love with the wild land and became "Adirondackers," a term used to denote the self-reliant and independent people who live in the Adirondacks year-round. In the mid-1800s such outdoor writers as Ned

Buntline and Charles Lawman wrote adventure-filled accounts of the colorful hunting and fishing guides of the north woods. These accounts attracted many sportsmen to the area, including Vice President Theodore Roosevelt.

Roosevelt's personality presented an interesting dichotomy because he was both an unequaled hunter yet, at the same time, one of the strongest supporters of wilderness protection. He was responsible for saving some of America's most cherished lands from the hands of unthinking developers and was a major force behind the early conservation movement.

North Creek still holds an attraction for outdoor adventurers with its many opportunities to experience the challenges of nature. One of the most exciting adventures is white-water rafting on the Hudson River. In the early spring, the river is flooded from the snow melt, and its rapids roar with the intensity of a storm-beaten ocean, creating waves several feet high.

I have taken a raft trip in the past, and there is nothing comparable to riding the crest of a thundering wave and then plunging down its backside into the foaming turmoil of a raging river. I remember how my river mates and I had to struggle to hold ourselves securely in the raft. We had battled through the Hudson River Gorge, which has almost continuous rapids for the first 3½ miles, then drops 150 feet near its end. But before we knew it, we had floated into calm water, shouting in triumph. While floating down the calm sections of river, we had time to enjoy the scenic views before we once again plunged into the swirling foam of the rapids. I remember that trip as if it were yesterday and wish I could have repeated it this tour, but it was midsummer and the river was too low. The raft trips usually run in the spring (when the river is wildest) and the fall. They are led by licensed guides, and all the necessary precautions are taken, but there is an element of risk. For the most part, though, it's safe and enjoyable for the entire family. Fishing, canoeing, and tubing (floating on a inner tube) are also great ways to enjoy the river as it flows alongside SR 28.

North Creek is the home of one of New York's best ski areas and the only one with a gondola ride to the summit. From its 3,600-foot summit, there are rewarding views of the vast, forested countryside. It's best to call ahead ([518] 251-2411) because off-season hours vary.

Into the Depths of a Garnet Mine

Although many of the industries in this region have died, the Barton Mines remain. Five miles north of North Creek off SR 28 on Barton Mine Road, the mines produce a major portion of the world's industrial garnets and still claim to be the largest garnet mines in the world. The open-pit mine area covers hundreds of acres. I visited a mineral shop, took the open-pit mine tour into the depths of the mine, and watched a slide show. Gem hunting is a favorite pastime of many visitors, and I must admit I became caught up in it myself, spending considerable time searching for garnets. There is a minimum charge for the two-hour tour, which includes the garnet hunting.

It was in the North Creek area, while on a hunting trip, that Roosevelt received word of President McKinley's death. He rushed from the wilderness to North Creek, taking the train from the North Creek Station to return to Washington to become the next president. The station still stands but, unfortunately, in disrepair.

Handful of Gems.
Industrial garnets like these are common finds for visitors touring the Barton Mines near North Creek.

Returning to SR 28, I continued west, stopping briefly in Indian Lake to browse through the Chimney Craftsmen, a wood furniture store with a stock of heavy wood tables, china cabinets, and other items of high quality and fine wood finishes—no veneers here. After visiting the store I continued across the Cedar River, noticing the turnoff for the Moose River Recreation Area. I realized I would be exiting from this point, after touring the Moose River area, near the end of my journey.

Sparkling Blue Mountain Lake

Adirondack Park encompasses forty-two mountains exceeding 4,000 feet, 2,800 lakes and ponds, 1,200 miles of rivers, and over 30,000 miles of brooks and streams. However, there are only 1,100 miles of highways and 1,200 miles of railroads.

By the time I arrived at Blue Mountain Lake, the name of both a lake and a small hamlet, it was late and I was tired, so I went directly to Golden Beach Public Campground. I decided the next day I would do three things: climb Blue Mountain, visit the Adirondack Museum, and drive to Buttermilk Falls and Forked Lake. This was an ambitious agenda, so I left at first light.

Climbing into the Heavens

Blue Mountain is one of the best climbs in the Adirondacks. It stands at 3,759 feet and commands overlooks of vast stretches of wilderness. The trail is approximately four miles round-trip, with a vertical rise of 1,750 feet. It isn't too difficult and can be climbed by the entire family. Hiking at a leisurely pace, with time at the summit, should require less than four hours to complete. The trailhead is located a mile or so north of the junction of SR 28 and SR 30, on SR 30 across from the Adirondack Museum.

I started at a good pace and brought plenty of water, since there is none on the trail. Only the steep final ascent presented any difficulty. But as I finally reached the summit, I was more thrilled with having conquered another peak than with the effort required to arrive here.

The best views are from the fire tower, which I immediately climbed. It's unique because it is one of the few remaining manned towers in the state, which, like so many others, is closing them in favor of using airplanes to spot fires.

From the Blue Mountain fire tower I was able to appreciate views which, according to guidebooks, include 165 Adirondack mountains and 16 lakes. The fire tower ranger helped me identify the surrounding peaks and bodies of water, including Raquette Lake, the Fulton Chain of Lakes, Terrel Pond, and even the High Peaks region.

Stepping into History at the Adirondack Museum

The Adirondack Museum, located on the site of a former hotel that operated from 1876 through 1956, is considered one of the best regional museums in the state. On a hill overlooking Blue Mountain Lake, the original log hotel, a two-story Colonial structure with a wooden clapboard porch, is part of the museum and open for viewing. Nearby is the original Ra-

Boat in a Bottle.
The sailboat *Water Witch*, enclosed in a plastic bubble, is one of the principal attractions at the Adirondack Museum near the village of Blue Mountain Lake.

quette Lake locomotive, used from 1900 to 1929 to carry passengers across the land between the lakes so they could travel from one boat to another without having to walk.

Each of the museum's twenty buildings depicts a different aspect of Adirondack life and history, from Colonial times to the present. Fifty-two freshwater boats and fifty-one horse-drawn vehicles used for both work and pleasure are on display. Most impressive was the *Oriental,* a railroad parlor car of mahogany and velvet, used to carry wealthy camp owners to the Adirondacks between 1891 and 1940. Exhibits on mining, rustic furniture, woods, hotels, famous camps, and clubs complete the museum's collection.

One of the most interesting displays is a photograph belt that continuously travels beneath a long glass table, displaying 160 historic photographs of famous guides, trappers, loggers, visitors, and landscapes. There are also two art galleries, with paintings from the museum's collection of famous Adirondack artists such as A. F. Tait, Winslow Homer, and Frederic Remington. In these same galleries, contemporary photographers show works that best capture the unique essence of the Adirondacks. Several hours passed before I realized that I still wanted to see Buttermilk Falls before dusk, so I left, heading north on SR 30.

Thundering Falls

The drive to Buttermilk Falls is a pretty one, and if you're a cyclist it makes a nice bike tour. The falls are actually more of a cascade, but are nonetheless a beautiful sight. As I relaxed at the water's edge, watching the plummeting falls, I noticed fishermen trying their luck a few yards below. Besides fishing, you can also picnic at this lovely location.

I drove on to Forked Lake Public Campground. This is not a campground for RVers; none of the sites are accessible by RV and all are tent sites only. Nevertheless, it is a nice place for a short stroll, and the lake is very pretty. I returned by the same route traveling south on SR 30 to Blue Mountain Lake and west on SR 28 back to Golden Beach Public Campground.

Buttermilk Falls.
More of a cascade than an actual waterfall, Buttermilk Falls is a bit difficult to find but is certainly worth the effort.

Courtesy of Finger Lakes State Parks Commission

Sweet Tooth.
A tiger swallowtail butterfly feeds on the nectar of wildflowers at Buttermilk Falls.

Touching the Wild at Raquette Lake

At Golden Beach I pulled into my campsite and started dinner. It had been a long, arduous day, and I was looking forward to relaxing in front of the fire. After dinner it was still quite warm, so I walked to the lake for a swim. Raquette Lake is extremely shallow, with a maximum depth of only ninety-six feet. The Golden Beach—South Bay area has a maximum depth of nineteen feet; you'd have to walk the equivalent of two city blocks out into the lake before reaching a depth of five feet, making it an optimum swimming beach if you're RVing with young children.

The name "Golden Beach" is an appropriate one because the sand is golden and in turn lends its color to the water. The beach is one of the finest in New York, with soft sand lapped by calm waters. The lake, one of the largest in the park, is perfect for boating; it covers 5,395 acres and has 90 miles of shoreline. There's excellent fishing with lake and brook trout, smallmouth bass, and yellow perch.

Sir John Johnson, a loyalist to King George III during the Revolution, was responsible for inadvertently giving Raquette Lake its name. He held a vast estate in the Mohawk Valley. In 1776, he decided to flee in hopes of fighting another day. He gathered together 170 of his tenants and their families and traveled toward Canada via the Adirondacks. To be on the safe side, even though it was May, they brought along snowshoes or "raquettes," as they were called. By the time they reached the lake, Johnson and his party realized the snowshoes were unnecessary, abandoned them on the shore, and proceeded by boat. The lake has been known as Raquette Lake ever since.

Bearly Visible.
This powerful black bear is generally a solitary animal, ambling along at a slow and steady rate but capable of bursts of speed up to 35 miles per hour.

The Adirondacks were not "discovered" until after the Civil War. Until then only loggers and hunters disturbed the wilderness. After the Civil War, however, it became the woodland retreat for the "great camps" of the rich and famous.

Close Encounters of a Bruin Kind

Feeling revived from my swim, I returned to camp and lit a fire as darkness slowly enveloped the forest. I prefer watching a fire in the dark and, consequently, very seldom use a lantern; this night was no exception. While gazing mindlessly at the flames, I suddenly felt an unheard presence. I disregarded it, but the feeling persisted and I reached for my flashlight, shining it into the woods. At first I saw only the underbrush, but then my beam homed in on the gleaming, jet-black fur of a huge bear. He lifted his gigantic head and his eyes glowed in the light; he grunted, and moved deeper into the forest. I breathed a sigh of relief and sat down in front of the fire. Shortly after that, I heard a roar in the darkness and a metallic crash from the hilltop where the "bear-proof" dumpsters are located. I heard another camper yell, "It's a bear!" Then things quieted down a bit, but not for long. Within a half hour, I felt a presence again and reached for my flashlight. Yes! It was another bear, but this one wasn't intimidated. He had discovered some food thrown away by some sloppy and inconsiderate campers and wasn't about to leave. He gave me a deep, low warning growl indicating he didn't appreciate a light shining in his face. Considering he was barely ten feet away, I deferred to his wishes and retreated.

Black bears, unlike their western cousins, the grizzlies, aren't usually aggressive. But nevertheless, it's necessary to take precautions and respect their power. The potential for danger is always there. The Adirondacks have a population of 3,600 bears; the average male adult weighs 300 pounds, but some have been known to reach 600 pounds. This region has a large share of the bear population, and most public campgrounds give out brochures detailing proper bear procedures. By following their suggestions, you can be assured of safety, and the bears will simply add to the adventure of camping in the Adirondacks. Besides bear, there is other wildlife in the area: beaver, coyote, bobcat, otter, and deer; some locals claim that wolves have returned. After a good night's rest, I was again on my way, traveling west on SR 28.

The Great Camps Era

The Sagamore Lodge is located a few miles west of Golden Beach and directly across from the turnoff for the hamlet of Raquette Lake. It's a bumpy, four-mile drive on a dirt-and-gravel road, but even the largest RVs can travel it easily. The Sagamore Lodge sits on the shore of the mile-long, pristine Sagamore Lake and is listed on the National Register of Historic Places. The lodge complex is surrounded by hundreds of thousands of acres of forest preserve and consists of twenty-nine buildings, many of them constructed of logs. William West Durant built the Sagamore in 1897 as a wilderness retreat. He is considered the most prominent builder of the Great Camps Era, a period in the late 1800s and early 1900s when the wealthy considered the Adirondacks their private campground, buying large tracts of land and then building expansive, rustic estates to serve as wilderness retreats.

Historic Sagamore.
Snug on the shore of a quiet wilderness lake, Sagamore Lodge is listed on the National Register of Historic Places. Constructed in 1897 as a private retreat, the lodge is now a conference and educational center.

Durant was only twenty-four when he became fascinated by the region and its potential. He immediately began a project to improve the transportation system into the wilderness and spent the next twenty-four years trying to complete it. His grandiose plans included selling off large portions of the family's massive land holdings to the very wealthy, so they could build estates with private lakes and hunting grounds, and smaller portions of land to well-to-do professionals and sportsmen. Durant, of course, planned to use his own railroad to ship supplies and artisans to develop the area.

Although Durant built several luxury camps in the Raquette Lake area, he was obsessed with Sagamore Lodge, upon which he lavished both money and personal attention. He was a notorious perfectionist. One time, discovering the porch was slightly out of kilter, he ordered it torn down and rebuilt. On another occasion, he discovered one stone in a major fireplace set incorrectly and ordered the masons to dismantle it and start all over. For more than twenty years, he employed 200 people to work on his camps and spent more than $250,000 on the main lodge of Sagamore alone.

In 1901, as a result of financial problems caused by extravagance and family disputes, Durant sold Sagamore to Alfred Vanderbilt, of the famous financial and industrial family. By 1904, he was financially ruined and was forced to clerk in a Newcomb hotel, serving many of the people he formerly employed. Durant, who had been one of the wealthiest men of his era, died penniless in New York City in the 1930s.

The Sagamore is now owned and operated by a nonprofit organization as a conference and educational center. Daily tours are conducted, lasting two hours including an interesting slide show and lecture on the Great Camps Era. Plans for the future include operating the Sagamore as it was when owned by Durant. There will be full-time artisans and craftspeople living and working on the premises, and their handmade Adirondack crafts will be for sale to visitors.

The tour led us through the grounds and into many beautiful, rustic, log buildings, with wooden walls and floors, great fireplaces, and detailed wood furniture. I was most taken with the main lodge, a three-story, chalet-style log structure containing turn-of-the-century furnishings and massive stone fireplaces. It's difficult to appreciate that Durant thought he was "roughing it" in this huge building. He even had an outdoor bowling alley (partially enclosed). I had the opportunity to play on it, and even after all these years it was as good as any modern facility.

Back on SR 28, I stopped briefly in tiny Raquette Lake (population 100), the epitome of a backwoods Adirondack town. There are a few houses, two churches, and a general store (open only through October), a bar, a launderette, post office, and a dock and marina. I felt as if I had stepped back into the 1940s as I entered the well-stocked general store, with its high ceilings, old lighting fixtures, and wooden floors.

Country Church.
Raquette Lake's St. William Catholic Church is the most prominent structure in this tiny mountain town.

Outside the general store, I was surprised to see an old acquaintance, Joe Guimara, an RVer from Maryland. I had met Joe and his family several years ago when camping in New York. While his wife, Virginia, and their daughter, Jennifer, shopped for supplies, we talked about the town. Joe told me, "If you think this is backwoods, drive to Stillwater. They have a population of twenty-five, and it's twelve miles over a dirt road to get there." He told me more about Stillwater and its reservoir, and I decided it would be worth a short side trip later.

Cruising along the Fulton Chain

The Fulton Chain of Lakes were named for Robert Fulton, inventor of the steamboat. He was commissioned by the New York State Legislature in 1811 to survey the central Adirondacks for a possible water route to Canada. The route proved impossible, but he wrote such glowing descriptions of the lakes along the way that they were referred to as Fulton's Chain Lakes or Fulton Chain of Lakes. The eight lakes run from Inlet to Old Forge and (with great imagination) have been named First Lake through Eighth Lake. The area offers beautiful scenery, swimming, fishing, boating, and extensive canoeing opportunities.

Gone Fishin'.
Waiting for the perch to bite, two youngsters intently watch their bobbers on 6th Lake.

A Town in the Wilderness

Inlet (population 320) is located at the head of Fourth Lake and is almost completely encircled by state-forest-preserve land. I stopped for a brief visit, walking through the town, looking in the stores and sitting on the beach, a lovely spot with huge pine trees and a pretty perspective of the lake. At Inlet, you can rent boats, ride horseback, fish, golf, or fly in a seaplane over the forest. I was going to take the seaplane ride, but my fear of flying overwhelmed my sense of adventure. The ride is highly recommended by several people I spoke to. Adirondack Discovery, a nonprofit organization that lectures about the Adirondacks, leads outings and hikes and provides numerous other free activities, is located in Inlet. You can receive an updated schedule of events by calling (315) 357-3598.

After touring Inlet, I continued west on SR 28 passing through Eagle Bay, a small town so named because a pair of nesting eagles once made the area their home. It is also the turnoff for Big Moose and Stillwater. Since I would be coming back this way, I decided to visit Stillwater on my return.

Up Bald Mountain

Halfway between Eagle Bay and Old Forge lies the Rondaxe Fire Tower Trail, an easy two-mile round-trip hike. I decided to hike it, and I enjoyed the panoramic view of the Fulton Chain of Lakes and hundreds of thousands of acres of forest wilderness. I was even lucky enough to spot one of the cruise boats from Old Forge making its way down the lakes. The trail has a few steep climbs but for the most part is easy and well worth the hour and a half it takes for a round trip.

Downtown Inlet.
There isn't much excitement in the small resort community of Inlet, but visitors seem to prefer it that way.

Peaceful Setting.
Flowers and benches give this private dock
on 6th Lake the look and feel of a sundeck.

Touring Old Forge

Charles Herreshoff, an early pioneer in the region, is responsible for giving Old Forge its name, although in a way he never intended. Herreshoff tried to establish a mining and farming community in the area but soon discovered settlers were unwilling to suffer the difficult work and harsh winters. He pinned his hopes on his lone iron mine, but a severe storm ruined the mine shaft, destroying Herreshoff's last hope for financial salvation. Realizing his dreams were over, he shot himself in the head. Without his motivating force, the settlers left, and his community reverted to wilderness. Hunters and trappers told stories about the remnants of Charles's old forge; the name became associated with the area and when a new community developed it called itself Old Forge, inadvertently becoming a monument to Charles's failed dream.

Today, Old Forge (population 1,500), although not a wilderness itself, is surrounded by one. As resident Ruth Giddings told me, "We still have a bear or two wander the streets on occasion, and in the winter deer are a common sight in town." Old Forge has quite a few attractions for RVers. The Enchanted Forest is fun for "kids" of all ages. They have several different shows daily, storybook attractions, a 400-foot tube ride on swirling white water, two 360-foot water chutes, and numerous other rides children will love.

McCauley Mountain Ski Center has lift rides to the summit and offers impressive vistas of the town, lakes, and surrounding wilderness. In town there are many stores that sell antiques, Adirondack crafts, and other items. I especially liked the Old Forge Woodmaker, which carries hand-made furniture, hand-decorated plates, paintings, and displays of works by local artisans.

I spent so much time browsing in the stores that I missed a ride on the double-decker cruise boat, the *Clearwater,* which travels the entire twenty-eight miles of the Fulton Chain. RVers who have made the cruise praised it highly, and I put it on my "must do" list for the next visit. I started back toward Eagle Bay, still planning to take a quick trip to Stillwater.

The Backwoods of Stillwater

Big Moose.
The tiny Adirondacks lake community of Big Moose is most famous as the locale of Theodore Dreiser's novel, *An American Tragedy.*

I traveled east on SR 28 to Eagle Bay and then made a left at the sign to Big Moose and Stillwater on CR 1; this road turns into Number Four (logging) Road. At Big Moose, the pavement ends. This is a small, backwoods lake

Backwoods Transportation.
The only way to get anywhere in a hurry in the rugged Adirondacks backwoods is by floatplane. These hardy aircraft are almost as common here as automobiles.

community, most famous for being the locale of Theodore Dreiser's novel, *An American Tragedy*. From here, it's twelve miles of dirt and gravel to Stillwater, another true backwoods Adirondack community. Although it has a population of only twenty-five, it provides many services to visitors: boat rentals, a grocery store, a gas station, and a hotel serving full-course meals. The present dam was constructed in 1925, and the reservoir, when full, covers 6,700 acres. The reservoir is surrounded by 158,240 acres of state-owned wilderness. The road is a bit rough with a few sandy spots, but for the most part can accommodate the largest motorhomes. In fact, I found the drive on the paved road to Big Moose more difficult because of its rolling and curving nature.

There are 117 miles of shoreline and 42 islands to explore. Seventeen miles of trails lead to trout streams, lakes, and other out-of-the-way places. Fishing is excellent with brook and lake trout and smallmouth bass.

At the first sight of the reservoir, I stopped to appreciate the view. I had been told that at Stillwater I would be able to see an even better view over the longest length of the lake. But a severe thunderstorm struck suddenly, darkening the sky and turning the road into muck. I tried to wait it out, but it didn't seem as if it would pass, so I decided it was better to head back.

Just outside of Big Moose, I saw a black bear walking down the road as if he owned it. He went for a big dumpster, totally disregarding the "Please Don't Feed the Bears" sign and started to feast. I parked my rig and watched until he had eaten his fill and retreated to the forest. I continued to SR 28, making a left, and heading east toward the Moose River Recreation Area.

Traveling the Wilderness Road of Moose River

Originally, I'd planned on camping at one of the primitive sites within the Moose River area, but due to the late hour and the inclement weather, I opted for spending the night at Limekiln Public Campground, off SR 28 near Inlet. The campground is attractive, with a lake and large, wooded, private sites.

The entrance to Moose River is just beyond Limekiln Lake; there is a ranger headquarters at the entrance. After signing in at the register, I picked up a map of the area, and plunged into the wilderness. The area offers RVers another opportunity to take advantage of their homes on wheels and experience backwoods camping. There's a main thirty-seven-mile dirt-and-gravel road, with many side roads leading to trailheads, lakes, streams, and ponds. The 50,000-acre Moose River Recreational Area is encircled by hundreds of thousands of acres of state wilderness. The terrain varies from the flatness of the Moose River Plain to the steep inclines of the adjoining mountains.

I found the road more than adequate for all types of RVs but you need to be completely self-contained to camp here, including your own water supply. The rewards are worth it; the area is very pretty and speckled with many primitive campsites possessing only a privy, picnic table, and fireplace. Most sites are large enough for RVs and spread a good distance apart from each other. Fishing, hunting, and trapping are allowed in season, and there are twenty-seven miles of hiking trails leading to ponds and lakes; some of the trails lead into the primitive West Canada Lake Wilderness area.

I bounced along the road, keeping to the fifteen-mile-per-hour speed limit and enjoying the surroundings. At the first stream crossing, I stopped to walk around and discovered a recently erected beaver dam. This area is teeming with bear, deer, coyote, loon, and hawk.

In a few areas, I noticed bear-claw marks on the trees and stopped to investigate. Some of the marks were over five feet high, which clearly indicated the size of the bear. They like to sharpen their claws on the trees by tearing across the bark, slicing the trees with the ease of a knife cutting through butter. I continued on the plain until I reached the Cedar River entrance; from here, it was a short drive over a paved road to SR 28 and the end of this tour.

Busy as a...
These nocturnal rodents live on the cambium layer (bark) of willow, cottonwood, and other trees. The Indians used the beaver for fur and for its glandular secretions purported to be medicinally useful. Thanks to conservation efforts, the once almost-extinct beaver is busy once again.

Lakeshore Camp.
This lovely traveler's park on the shores of Indian Lake attracts many RVers.

At this point, you have the option of extending the tour by not returning to Warrensburg and I-87 but instead taking a scenic drive south on SR 30 to New York Thruway 90. The drive is lovely, with more mountain views, small towns, and lakes. I traveled this route so I could climb Pillsbury Mountain, an easy, panoramic hike. The entrance is at Mason Lake, about nineteen miles south of the town of Indian Lake and then about five miles on a dirt logging road to the trailhead. There are a few primitive camping sites on the shores of Mason Lake that RVers use.

I once backpacked from here deep into the West Canada Lake Wilderness and saw remnants of French Louie's fireplace, the only completed part of his planned wilderness inn. French Louie was a notorious Adirondack character who lived on the shores of West Lake for more than forty years, hunting, trapping, logging, and guiding visitors through the region.

Indian Lake.
Indian Lake, with its fish-filled waters, is just one of many natural impoundments that dot the Adirondacks.

When Verplank Colvin wanted to survey the area, French Louie offered his expertise as a guide. But Colvin only hired Republicans; Louie, a Democrat, was disqualified. Colvin, however, did want to rent Louie's boats and thereby gave Louie an opportunity for revenge. Louie told him his boats were Democrats, too, and refused to rent them to Colvin.

It's worth the time to spend an extra day or two in the Speculator area. There are more than fourteen lakes within a radius of fifteen miles, and the public beach offers picturesque views of the lake and Speculator Mountain. Six campgrounds provide bases from which you can fish, boat, hike, or golf (check your *Trailer Life Campground & RV Services Directory* for more complete information).

As I left Speculator and drove south, my Adirondack tour had come to an end. I had to say good-bye, for now, to this unique, immense state park. But I knew that more adventure and excitement awaited me on the road.

POINTS OF INTEREST: New York Tour 3

The Central Adirondacks

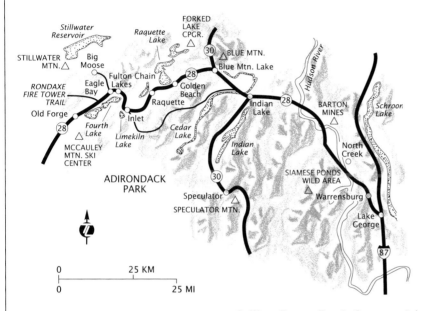

ACCESS: *New York Thruway Interstate 87 to exit 23 to Warrensburg, west on SR 28.*

INFORMATION: *Hamilton County Publicity Bureau,* Long Lake, 12847 (518) 624-4151; *Central Adirondack Association,* Old Forge, 13420 (315) 369-6983; *Warrensburg Chamber of Commerce,* Box 382, 12885 (518) 623-2161; *Inlet Chamber of Commerce Arrowhead Park,* Inlet, 13360 (315) 357-5501.

ANNUAL EVENTS:

Warrensburg: *Antiques Market* (over a hundred dealers), August; *Fall Foliage & World's Largest Garage Sale,* October.

Blue Mountain Lake: *Benefit Auction,* July; *Craftspeople at Work* (snowshoes, wood-canvas canoes, rustic furniture, packbasket, Akwesasne baskets) July through August.

Old Forge: *Father's Day Frog Jumping Contest,* June; *International Festival, Central Adirondack Craft Fair,* July; *Regional Adirondack Art Show,*

Sailing Races, Band Concerts, July through August.

Speculator: *Outdoor Flea Market,* July; *Concert at the Gazebo,* August.

MUSEUMS AND GALLERIES:

Warrensburg: *Historical Museum,* 47 Main Street (518) 623-2928. June—September, Wednesday—Sunday 12 P.M. to 5 P.M.

Blue Mountain Lake: *Adirondack Museum,* State Routes 28N and 30 (518) 352-7311. May through October, 10 A.M. to 6 P.M.; *Adirondack Lakes Center for the Arts,* State Routes 28 and 30 (518) 352-7715, artist presentations, arts, crafts, concerts, June—September, 9 A.M.—5 P.M.

Old Forge: *The Hand of Man,* Main Street (315) 369-3381, crafts and watercolors; *Town of Webb Historical Museum,* Crosby Boulevard (315) 369-3838, all year Monday, Wednesday, and Friday 9 A.M.—5 P.M.

OUTFITTERS:

Blue Mountain Lake Guide Service, Box 111, Blue Mountain Lake 12812 (518) 352-7684.

Adirondack Range Guide and Outfitter, Box 8, Hoffmeister 13353 (315) 826-7416.

RESTAURANTS:

Warrensburg: *Anthony's Italian Restaurant* (518) 623-2162; homemade Sicilian-style cuisine.

Inlet: *The Mountaineer* (315) 357-3498; American cuisine.

Big Moose: *Big Moose Inn* (315) 357-2042; American cuisine.

Old Forge: *Riverside Restaurant* (315) 369-6582; Italian cuisine; *Old Mill Restaurant* (315) 369-3662; prime beef and seafood specialties.

SPECIAL ATTRACTIONS:

Inlet: *Bird's Seaplane Service,* Sixth Lake, Inlet, 13360 (315) 357-3631; *Payne's Air Service,* Seventh Lake, Inlet, 13360 (315) 357-3971.

Old Forge: Boat cruises aboard the *Clearwater* and *Uncas,* Old Forge, 13420 (315) 369-6473; *McCauley Mountain Ski Center,* Old Forge, 13420 (315) 369-6983, chair lift rides to the summit for panoramic views; *Enchanted Forest,* SR 28, Old Forge, 13420 (315) 369-6145, rides, shows, and games; open daily Memorial Day weekend through Labor Day, 9:30 A.M. to 5:30 P.M.

North Creek: *Barton Mines Corporation Garnet Mine,* Barton Mine Road, North Creek, 12853 (518) 251-2706. Open daily June 25 through Labor Day, 9 A.M. to 4 P.M.; *Whitewater Rafting Trips on the Hudson River,* North Creek, 12853 (518) 251-3215, March 28—May 31 and September 19—October 12, departures 8 A.M., Friday—Sunday.

Raquette Lake: *Great Camp Sagamore* (Sagamore Lodge and Conference Center), off SR 28, Sagamore Road, Raquette Lake, 13436 (315) 354-5311, tours, programs, educational workshops, and crafts, open daily year-round, 9 A.M.—5 P.M.

The Hudson Valley

When power leads man toward arrogance, poetry reminds him of his limitations. When power narrows the areas of man's concern, poetry reminds him of the richness and diversity of his existence. When power corrupts, poetry cleanses, for art establishes the basic human truths which must serve as the touchstone of our judgment.

John F. Kennedy,
address at Amherst College, October 10, 1963

The Hudson River Valley, in eastern New York, runs north from the New Jersey border to Albany, bordered on the west by the Catskill Mountains and on the east by Connecticut and Massachusetts. It's a lush land of farms, wineries, mountains, small towns, and great estates. If there ever was an eastern plutocratic establishment, it was here on the highlands overlooking the banks of the Hudson River that they made their homes. In many cases, these American aristocratic families have moved on to trendier locations, and now many of their former estates are in the public domain. I was looking forward to visiting several of these great estates.

Albany

Tour **4** *129 miles*

SUGAR LOAF • WEST POINT • BEAR MOUNTAIN STATE PARK • ROOSEVELT NATIONAL HISTORIC SITE • VANDERBILT MANSION • STAATSBURG • RHINEBECK • CLERMONT STATE HISTORIC SITE AND PARK • OLANA STATE HISTORIC SITE AND PARK

The Craftspeople of Sugar Loaf

I began my tour in the lovely Wallkill Valley at the crafts village of Sugar Loaf, nestled amid farmland, apple orchards, horse farms, and mountains. Nearby country roads could be fun to explore.

Sugar Loaf was established as a leading crafts center in 1968, but the hamlet's history dates back to 1749 when the first white settlers arrived. The town was built in the shadow of Sugar Loaf Mountain on a site that was once an Indian burial ground. The town grew and prospered and by the early 1800s had three inns and taverns, a cheese factory, soap factory, church, and school. The growing railroad industry funneled development to other areas and Sugar Loaf evolved into a residential community. But during the sixties, drawn by the beauty and inexpensive housing and shops, many craftspeople came to the small town. Today, there are forty craftspeople, and more than twenty-six shops housed in original eighteenth- and nineteenth-century buildings.

You can while away a few enjoyable hours in Sugar Loaf. I especially liked two shops. The Exposures Gallery is devoted exclusively to original photography. Nick Zungoli, the owner, is a well-known photographer and displays his own work as well as work of other respected photographers. Zungoli's photos, many of them landscapes, evoke a feeling for the land, whether it's a mountain fiery with fall colors or a meadow glistening in the summer sun. Caribou Canyon is a leather-goods store that features handmade belts, jackets, and sandals; custom orders are accepted.

Additional shops specialize in wood furniture, jewelry, wood carvings, stained glass, pottery, and other country crafts—quilts, prints, rag dolls, and candles. The Barnsider Tavern, a good place to eat, is a converted barn with a rustic atmosphere; soups, salads, and hot and cold sandwiches are served. Most of the shops are open Wednesday through Saturday from 11 A.M. to 6 P.M. For a complete listing of dates, times, and cultural events write Sugar Loaf Crafts Guild, P.O. Box 125, Sugar Loaf, New York 10981 (914) 469-4963.

Reflections.
Mirrored in the slow-moving waters of small creek, this stone cottage is one of several attractive buildings visitors can tour at the Eleanor Roosevelt National Historic Site.

Pasture Perfection.
A well-tended white rail fence surrounds the pastures and outbuildings of this elegant horse ranch near Sugarloaf.

After visiting the shops, I continued north on CR 13 (King's Highway) to the intersection of CR 13 and SR 17M; I made a right and traveled for several miles until I spotted the Museum Village of Orange County in Monroe and decided to stop for a brief visit.

Walking into a Rural Past

The museum complex includes thirty buildings with over 25,000 objects exemplifying rural life in Orange County during the nineteenth century. A blacksmith shop, log smoke house, general store, stove museum, and cedar mill help to bring the era alive. Massive sections of chestnut trees in the building house the farm tool exhibit—four sections of trees serve as columns holding up the front of the structure; inside you can see several more sections. The trees, some over twenty feet in circumference, were killed by a blight during the 1800s.

I also enjoyed the Natural History Museum's mastodon. Remains of this extinct relative of the elephant have been found in Orange County. Both Thomas Jefferson and George Washington visited the area in the 1800s to see these mastadon relics. The museum also features special events, such as nineteenth-century magic acts, children's theater, and square dancing. Call (914) 782-8247 for an updated events schedule.

Leaving the museum, I continued east on SR 17M, which connects with SR 17, where I turned north to the junction with SR 6, then right, heading northeast. I continued on SR 6 to SR 293, taking it north to West Point Military Academy.

Sounding Cadence at West Point

West Point is America's oldest military post in continuous operation, as well as its oldest military academy. In 1778, General Washington, realizing the strategic importance of the location, ordered a permanent garrison of Revolutionary troops stationed here. Learning from his experiences during the war, and aware of the need for a professionally trained officer corps, President Thomas Jefferson created the military academy on March 16, 1802.

For over 185 years, the academy has trained American military leaders. In spite of the uniformity demanded of military personnel, some of the nation's most brilliant, individualistic, and flamboyant generals have been West Point graduates, including Generals Custer, Lee, MacArthur, and Patton. The first class numbered a mere ten; today, there are approximately

West Point.
Sprawling across a tree-blanketed hillside overlooking the Hudson River, West Point is America's oldest military academy.

Future Officers and Gentlemen.
Army cadets ready themselves for morning formation on West Point's main parade ground.

4,400 cadets. The academic curriculum includes a core of liberal arts, social sciences, engineering, and sciences, as well as electives. Along with the academics, military training covers all areas demanded by modern warfare. Upon graduation, cadets receive bachelor of science degrees and are commissioned as second lieutenants in the regular army.

I drove my rig into the museum parking lot overlooking the Hudson River. The paved lot actually serves as the roof for several structures built into the highlands above the river, affording a sweeping vista of the river, the valley, and the Point twenty feet above the treetops that grow along the shoreline. The stone edifices of West Point appear as medieval castles outlined against the horizon. To my right, the green grass of the Plain spread toward the curve of the river, and the mountains on the eastern shore rose like fortress walls.

The museum is said to have one of the largest collections of military artifacts in the western hemisphere: weapons, paintings, and exhibits from wars date back to the time of the Roman Empire. I was most interested in the World War II exhibits, including a Walther semi-automatic pistol that belonged to Heinrich Himmler, chief of the SS, and pistols that belonged to the other Nazi butchers, Hitler, Goering, and Goebbels.

After the museum, I strolled along the perimeter of the Plain, where statues honoring Generals Patton, Eisenhower, and MacArthur have been erected. I recalled how MacArthur once referred to Eisenhower, who served under him in the Philippines, as "the best clerk I ever had," and Eisenhower recalling that same tour of duty said of MacArthur, "I studied dramatics under him."

There are several chapels for the cadets, but one of the most impressive is Cadet Chapel on Mills Road. The large stone structure features beautiful stained-glass windows and is noted for having one of the largest church organs in the world. The organ is made up of 18,000 pipes, ranging in size from one smaller than a pen to some 32 feet long and weighing 500 pounds.

I left via the south gate, where there is a visitor center, taking SR 218 south to SR 9W and south toward Bear Mountain Bridge. At the bridge, I continued south to Bear Mountain State Park.

On Top of Bear Mountain

Spread out over 5,000 acres, Bear Mountain State Park offers miles of trails, a small zoo, a swimming pool, a lake for boating, a winter ice-skating rink, and picnic areas. In the summer months, due to the proximity to New York City (forty miles away), it can become excessively crowded. But during the off-season it's a more pleasant place to visit.

I followed the signs to Perkins Memorial Drive, which winds its way to the summit of Bear Mountain. Expansive views on the way up include one of the Bear Mountain Bridge spanning the Hudson River from one mountain to another, a spectacular sight. From the summit of the mountain, I could see a vast section of the Hudson River Valley, mountains, the river, and even the tips of New York City's skyscrapers peeking above the mountaintops. An observation tower, open during the summer, offers better views than the summit itself.

Leaving Bear Mountain, I returned to SR 9W, taking it north to the Bear Mountain Bridge. Crossing the Hudson, I made a left onto SR 9D, and proceeded north to Cold Spring.

Cold Spring is a national historic district with many notable examples of nineteenth-century buildings and a good view of the Hudson at the end of Main Street. Tours are conducted by appointment (call [914] 264-2111). I traveled east on SR 301 to Clarence Fahnestock State Park for the night, where RVers can camp, fish, and hike.

First thing in the morning, I drove west on SR 301 to US 9, then north to Hyde Park (population 2,500), home to three elaborate mansions, including Franklin D. Roosevelt National Historic Site, my first stop.

Visit to a President's Home

The Roosevelt estate epitomizes the charm and elegance of the pre-World War II Hudson Valley aristocracy. The historic site is made up of Roosevelt's home, presidential library, museum, and 200 acres of land. A

Impressive Artwork.
Stained-glass windows grace the beautiful West Point Cadet Chapel.

Crossing the Hudson.
Bear Mountain Bridge, spanning the Hudson River forty miles from New York City, is an engineering masterpiece.

Victorian-style house was built in 1826 and purchased by FDR's father in 1867. Here at Springwood, the family's name for the estate, Franklin was born in 1882. Enlarged and redesigned in neo-Georgian style in 1915, the home remains basically the same as it was at FDR's death in 1945: an impressive two-story structure of stone and mortar exterior with four white columns at its main entrance and large colonial-style windows throughout. Both Franklin and Eleanor are buried in the rose garden, the mounds of their graves plainly visible in front of a white marble monument.

Before entering the museum, I walked around the estate, admiring the tall trees and the Hudson River. The museum houses memorabilia from FDR's life, including his presidential desk, gifts from world leaders, and photographs.

The presidential library displays items of interest to scholars and the general public alike. There are 15,000,000 manuscript pages and documents bequeathed by Roosevelt to the American people, as well as 40,000 books, including 15,000 from the President's personal library. There's also a large collection of audiovisual material and photographs including his private collection of material on the United States Navy, the history of Dutchess County, and the Hudson Valley.

A tree-lined path leads to the thirty-four-room mansion and into the main entrance with its dark, heavy wood trim, doors, and bookcases. An eighteenth-century grandfather clock, purchased by the Roosevelts in Europe in 1881, stands against a picture-covered wall in the main hall.

To the right is the extensive servants' wing, occupying two floors. These eight bedrooms, trunk room, sewing room, three bathrooms, and valet room are not open to the public. The number of servants varied, but usually included a cook, parlor maid, butler, second man, footman, laundress, and kitchen maid. FDR's office is also located in the servants' wing and can be observed through a window from the outside. He called this room his summer White House, and it was here on June 20, 1942, that British Prime Minister Winston Churchill and the President signed the agreement to manufacture the first atomic bomb.

From the main hall, I could see the dining room and the Dresden Room (so named because of its Dresden chandelier and mantel purchased in Germany in 1866 by Roosevelt's father); the Snuggery, his mother's sitting and reading room; and the spacious living room. Most of the rooms are

President's Home.
The Franklin D. Roosevelt Mansion was constructed in 1826 and is now one of the Hudson River Valley's most popular tourist attractions.

Roosevelt Memorial.
Located in a peaceful garden setting adjacent to the mansion, the graves of Franklin and Eleanor Roosevelt repose amidst the flowers they both loved.

trimmed with dark wood and, despite their large dimensions, feel warm and homey.

On the second floor, I peeked into Roosevelt's tiny boyhood bedroom and the larger bedrooms with beautiful estate views. Leaving the mansion from the back exit, I looked across the green lawn, the huge old trees, and the view across the Hudson River, all of which made me feel as if I were on a European baronial estate.

I wanted to see the Eleanor Roosevelt National Historic Site, so I took the shuttle bus from Springwood, the only way to get there. This was Eleanor's retreat from the duties of her public life, and where she lived after Franklin died. The restored home features a film biography and a guided tour. Visitors can explore the grounds on hiking trails. It's interesting to contrast the relative simplicity of her residence with the opulence of her husband's mansion. Having completed my tour, I proceeded north on SR 9 to the Vanderbilt Mansion National Historic Site.

A Gilded Age Mansion

The Vanderbilt mansion is magnificent, even more so when you realize it was just a summer home. The Italian Renaissance-style structure was built in 1898 and has fifty rooms on four levels, set on a vast expanse of scenic grounds. Frederick Vanderbilt made it his country home for forty-three years until his death in 1938. He was the grandson of world-famous Cornelius "The Commodore" Vanderbilt, railroad baron, owner of the New York Central Railroad, and one of the world's richest men.

The mansion is described as a "modest" example of the Gilded Age, a time when the rich went to great lengths to display their wealth, especially in their homes. I was overwhelmed by the opulence of the mansion and the beauty of 211 acres of grounds. The total cost of the estate was estimated at $2,250,000, at a time when the average wage earner made a dollar a day.

As I entered the house between gigantic two-story columns into the reception hall and stood under a twenty-foot ceiling and three-story skylight, I recalled with amusement that younger members of the large Vanderbilt clan referred to this place as "Uncle Freddy's little cottage on the Hudson" because it was the smallest of the Vanderbilt estates.

The corniches and pilasters of the reception hall are green and white marble imported from Italy. Many items throughout the room are hundreds of years old, including a Flemish tapestry with the insignia of the famous Italian-Renaissance Medici family and two French Renaissance tooled-walnut cabinets. And, as if in acknowledgment of their aristocratic pretensions, there are two high-backed Italian throne chairs.

Each room is more impressive than the previous one, but I like the dining room the most. Its thirty-by-fifty-foot floor is almost completely covered by a 300-year-old oriental rug. Most of the furnishings are reproductions of the Louis XIV period, including the dining table that seats thirty.

Gem of the Gilded Age.
Almost unbelievably, the magnificent, fifty-room Vanderbilt Mansion was used only as a summer home.

In its heyday, the estate had a staff of sixty full-time employees. The "little cottage" was completely self-sufficient, with its own powerhouse, cattle, produce, chickens, and other animals to supply all its needs. Returning to my rig, I took US 9 north to Staatsburg, turning left onto Old Post Road.

The Country Charm of Staatsburg

Staatsburg is thought to be the earliest settlement in the Hyde Park area. Named for Dr. Samuel Staats of New York City, who lived here from 1715 to 1720, the hamlet grew because of the commerce generated by the estates and farms in the region. One of the most beautiful buildings in Staatsburg is St. Margaret Episcopal Church. An English Gothic adaptation with French medieval stained-glass windows, this impressive bell-towered stone structure was erected in the mid-1800s. An appointment is needed to visit the church. Call (914) 471-0406 and Eugene O'Dell, the warden, will be happy to arrange a tour. I continued on Old Post Road to Mills-Norrie State Park, which offers camping, fishing, hiking trails, and a boat launch for access to the Hudson River.

St. Margaret Church.
Erected in the mid-1800s, the English-Gothic St. Margaret Episcopal Church in Staatsburg is one of the area's most impressive religious structures.

Another Mansion of the Gilded Age

The Mills Mansion, part of Mills-Norrie State Park, is similar in style, content, and grandeur to the Vanderbilt estate. Morgan Lewis, a Revolutionary colonel and third governor of New York state, built his home on this site in 1792. Through marriage, the estate passed to the Livingston family, and then to Ruth Livingston. She married Ogden Mills, a wealthy financier who made his money during the California gold rush.

In 1895, Mills hired an architectural firm to remodel and enlarge the structure, creating a mansion modeled after many European estates. Some of its sixty-five rooms are decorated with ornamental gilt and oak paneling, and many of its original furnishings are in the styles of Louis XV and Louis XVI. The exterior is being renovated and is expected to be completed by 1995, but I still recommend a visit. After my tour, I followed Old Post Road north until it connected with US 9 and continued north on US 9 to Rhinebeck.

Barnstorming Days in Rhinebeck

The picturesque village of Rhinebeck (population 2,500) was incorporated in 1834 and claims to have one of the oldest inns in America still in operation, the Beekman Arms (1766). It has been a meeting place for some of the nation's greatest leaders; Presidents Washington to Franklin Roosevelt. General Lafayette and Alexander Hamilton, along with many other Revolutionary leaders, spent many days planning their strategies at the Beekman. In later years, Horace Greeley and William Jennings Bryan were also guests.

Needless to say, I was drawn to the Beekman and decided it was only fitting that I lift a mug of ale to honor all its historic guests. The inn still maintains much of its nineteenth-century charm. Outside, large columns rise two stories and Colonial windows and doors grace the facade; the inside features broad mellowed beams and planks in the ceiling. There was a cozy fire crackling in the waiting room, scenting it with the fragrant aroma of burning wood. Low ceilings and paneled walls are decorated with historical mementos: corncob pipes, muskets, swords, powder horns, maps, and pistols. There's a rustic tap room and several dining rooms. I didn't eat here but the quality of the cuisine is reportedly superb.

Continuing north on US 9, I turned right onto Stone Church Road to the Old Rhinebeck Aerodrome, the location of a weekend air show. It has the feel of the old barnstorming days with its dirt and grass parking lot, rustic food booths, and wooden bleachers overlooking the field. The Old Rhinebeck Aerodrome is a living museum of airplanes, covering the Pioneer, World War I, and the Lindbergh eras of aviation. Buildings are filled with historic planes, cars, motorcycles, and other vehicles. The best time to visit is on the weekend, when you can see many of these old planes fly.

The show, which runs from 2:30 to 4 P.M., was in progress as I made my way to the field. The Red Baron's triplane, a blood-red Fokker, was roaring through the sky with a 1916 Sopwith Pup biplane in hot pursuit. As soon as they raced by, a biwinged Sopwith Camel dove from the sky, dropping hand-held bombs on the "enemy" below. A fire exploded in one of the buildings; firemen in an antique fire truck raced across the field to fight the blaze. In the midst of all the excitement, a blow-by-blow account of the raging battle was broadcast over the loudspeakers.

A World War I tank joined the ground forces by attacking an armored car and battling the planes. Pilots in full uniform were continuously landing and taking off, all relishing the sense of adventure of flying these old planes and living the romance of a bygone era.

I enjoyed the show in spite of its sometimes corny nature and was equally enchanted with the planes on the ground. If you want to be a daredevil, barnstorming rides in a 1929 open-cockpit biplane are available

World War I fighter pilots often personalized their aircraft by painting names or designs on the noses of their planes. One such plane at the Old Rhinebeck Aerodrome, a reproduction of a 1916 Royal Air Force F. E. 8, features a large shark's face, complete with teeth, on the nose.

before and after the show. The ride takes you across the Hudson Valley sky and allows you to see the river, farms, and mountains from an unparralleled perspective. Weather conditions can affect the show, so it's best to call (914) 758-8610 beforehand.

I returned to US 9, traveling north to SR 199, turning east until SR 9G, then north toward Olana State Historic Site. The drive along SR 9G is beautiful; the Catskill Mountains lift regally several thousand feet from the Hudson Valley floor, and lush farmland lies below. There are several antique stores and country churches along the route, and several farms invite you to pick your own produce. On my way toward Olana, I spotted Clermont State Park and decided to stop.

Clermont State Historic Site and Park

The Livingston Mansion is the centerpiece of Clermont State Park, set alongside the Hudson River amid some of the better views of the Catskill Mountains and the Hudson River. Picnicking, hiking, and biking are popular here.

Robert R. Livingston was a patriot, scientist, statesman, member of the committee that drafted the Declaration of Independence, and the negotiator of the Louisiana Purchase.

His home was originally erected in 1730 but burned by British forces in 1777. Rebuilt during the late eighteenth century, the three-story colonial mansion is now open for guided tours. I was able to see hundreds of antiques gathered during the Livingston family's 200 years of occupancy.

As I walked the grounds, I spotted an historic marker designating the site of the Clermont Dock. Robert Livingston had helped to design and finance Robert Fulton's North River steamboat, the *Clermont,* and it had anchored here on its maiden voyage from New York City to Albany.

The Livingstons were overachievers by any century's standards. Robert R. Livingston's father was a prominent New York jurist. Great-grandfather and founder of the dynasty, Robert Livingston established the estate of 160,000 acres and was also U.S. Secretary of Indian Affairs. Brother Edward was, among other things, a member of the U.S. House of Representatives and a U.S. Senator.

An Artist's Mansion

Olana State Historic Site, off SR 9G, was once the home of Frederick E. Church (1826–1900), famed artist of the Hudson River School of painting. He studied under Thomas Cole and was one of the most famous of these nineteenth-century American landscape painters. Olana, a Persian-style villa, is a work of art itself, sitting on top of a mountain overlooking the northern expanse of the Hudson River Valley. The villa is a multilevel wood and stone structure with several towers, porches, and intricate exterior designs and colors emphasizing its Middle Eastern architecture.

Although I was able to walk around the villa and admire it from various angles, I had arrived too late for the last tour that starts at 4 P.M. I was told

Barnstorming Again.
An antique airplane from the famous Rhinebeck Aerodrome flies slowly over the Hudson River Valley. Weekend airshows featuring a fleet of these old planes attract visitors to Rhinebeck from all over the United States.

Olana on the Hudson.
Once the home of noted artist Frederic Church, this Persian-style mansion lies in the heart of Olana State Historic Site.

that an extensive collection of superb landscape paintings by Church, imported decorative arts, intricate wall stencils, and carved furniture are on display. Reservations for tours can be made by calling (518) 828-0135. The grounds are open for walking, picnicking, and, in the winter, cross-country skiing and ice skating.

Olana was the end of my tour this time, but I recommend taking a cruise on the Hudson River, which I have done in the past. It greatly enhanced my appreciation of this magnificent river that flows 315 miles from the Adirondack Mountains to New York City. There are several locations along the river where cruises are offered.

I watched the sun disappear behind the escarpment of the Catskill Mountains, its last dying rays painting the river a subdued orange. I couldn't help but agree with those who have called the Hudson River "America's Rhine." We may not have castles, but our great estates, vineyards, farms, small towns, and mountains that line the shore are certainly as impressive and beautiful.

POINTS OF INTEREST: New York Tour 4

The Hudson Valley

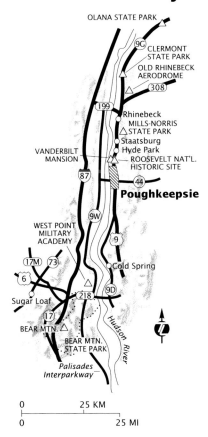

OLANA STATE PARK
9G CLERMONT STATE PARK
OLD RHINEBECK AERODROME
308
199
Rhinebeck
MILLS-NORRIS STATE PARK
Staatsburg
Hyde Park
VANDERBILT MANSION
ROOSEVELT NAT'L. HISTORIC SITE
87
44
Poughkeepsie
9W
WEST POINT MILITARY ACADEMY
9
17M 73
Cold Spring
6
218 9D
Sugar Loaf
17
BEAR MTN.
BEAR MTN. STATE PARK
Hudson River
Palisades Interparkway

0   25 KM
0   25 MI

ACCESS: *New York Thruway (87) to exit 16,* west on *State Highway 17 to* Chester, south on *CR 13.*

INFORMATION: *Hudson River Valley Association,* 72 Main Street, Cold Spring-on-Hudson, 10516 (914) 265-3066; *New York State Department of Commerce,* Division of Tourism, One Albany Avenue, Kingston, 12401 (914) 331-6415; *Dutchess County Tourism Promotion Agency,* P.O. Box 2025, 46 Albany Post Road, Hyde Park, 12538 (914) 229-0033; *Orange County Tourism,* 124 Main Street, Goshen, 10924 (914) 294-5151.

ANNUAL EVENTS:

Rhinebeck: *Crafts Fair,* June; *Auction and Antique Show,* July; *Dutchess County Fair,* August.

Croton: *Clearwater Hudson River Revival,* folk festival, music, crafts, June.

Garrison: *Arts and Crafts Fair,* August.

Staatsburg: *A Day in The Park,* music, games, crafts, antique carriage show, Mills Memorial State Park, August.

Tuxedo: *New York Renaissance Festival,* August through September.

MUSEUMS AND GALLERIES:

Monroe: *Museum Village in Orange County,* SR 17M (914) 782-8247, nineteenth-century rural village, exhibits, special events, May through November, Wednesday—Friday 10 A.M.—5 P.M., Saturday and Sunday noon—5 P.M.

West Point: *Military Museum,* Thayer Road (914) 938-2638, war exhibits, daily year-round, 10:30 A.M.—4:15 P.M.

Hyde Park: *Franklin D. Roosevelt National Historic Site Library and Museum,* SR 9 (914) 229-9115, year-round daily, 9 A.M.—5 P.M., closed major holidays and Tuesday and Wednesday, December through February; *Vanderbilt Mansion National Historic Site,* US 9 (914) 229-9115, hours and dates same as Roosevelt Historic Site.

Staatsburg: *Mills Mansion,* Albany Post Road (914) 889-4100, paintings, period furnishings, Oriental objects, May through Labor Day, Wednesday to Saturday 10 A.M.—5 P.M., Sunday 1—5 P.M., after Labor Day through October, Wednesday through Sunday noon—5 P.M.

Rhinebeck: *Old Rhinebeck Aerodrome Museum,* Old Stone Church Road (914) 758-8610, old planes, cars, motorcycles, air show and rides, daily, mid-May through October 10 A.M.—5 P.M., Saturday and Sunday air shows, 2:30—4 P.M.

Germantown: *Clermont State Historic Park—Livingston Mansion,* off SR 9G (914) 537-4240, period furnishings, paintings, exhibits, late May through October, Wednesday—Saturday 10 A.M. —5 P.M., Sunday 1 P.M.—5 P.M.

SPECIAL ATTRACTIONS:

Hudson River Cruises: *Hudson Highland Cruises & Tours, Inc.,* P.O. Box 265, Highland Falls, 10928 (914) 446-7171, dinner cruise, historic narration, and private charters; *Hudson River Cruises,* 524 North Ohioville Road, New Paltz (914) 255-6515, narrated cruise from Kingston and West Point; *Shearwater Cruises and Sailing School, Inc.,* RD 2, Box 329, Rhinebeck 12572 (914) 876-7350, boat charters and sailing lessons from Norrie Point Marina.

OUTFITTERS:

Hogancamp Guide Service, P.O. Box 565, Old Post Road, Marlboro, 12542 (914) 236-4131.

Timothy Hinkley, Wilderness Guide Services, P.O. Box 93, Halcottsville, 12438 (607) 326-7606.

RESTAURANTS:

Sugar Loaf: *Sugar Loaf Inn,* CR 13 (King's Highway) (914) 469-2552; country inn, local wines, American cuisine.

West Point: *Hotel Thayer* (914) 446-4731; grand old hotel, river views, American cuisine.

Cold Spring: *Dockside Harbor Restaurant,* One North Street (914) 256-3503; seafood.

Hyde Park: *Springwood Inn,* SR 9 (914) 229-2681; American cuisine.

Rhinebeck: *Beekman Arms,* SR 9 (914) 876-7077; American cuisine.

New Paltz: *Locust Tree Inn,* 215 Huguenot Street (914) 255-7888; country dining in a 1759 stone house; *Mohonk Mountain House,* Lake Mohonk (914) 255-1000; national historic landmark, American cuisine.

The Catskill Mountains

Friends of my heart, lovers of Nature's works,
Let me transport you to those wild blue mountains
That rear their summits near Hudson's wave
Though not the loftiest that begirt the land,
They yet sublimely rise, and on their heights
Your souls may have a sweet foretaste of heaven,
and traverse wide the boundless . . .

Thomas Cole,
Guide to the Catskills

Long before I exited from the Thruway (I-87) to begin my tour of Catskill State Park, I could see the Catskill Mountains above the Hudson Valley. The park is located in southeastern New York, about three hours north of New York City. Its more than 700,000 acres cover over half the land in four counties. Designated "forever wild," 272,000 acres of forest must be kept in their natural state; the rest of the park is interspersed with development. The Catskills have some of the best trout streams in the state and wild white water for canoeing, rafting, and tubing. There are numerous scenic drives, miles of hiking trails, ski resorts, covered bridges, and even a Buddhist monastery and retreat.

I left I-87 at exit 19, driving west on SR 28 toward Woodstock, eight miles ahead. I decided to stop at the Catskill Mountain Antique Center, a rustic two-story clapboard building. It is only one of many antique stores in the Catskills, but if you are a collector, I recommend this one. They have an array of old guns, paintings, lanterns, clothing, and furniture with an authentic country flavor. After satisfying my curiosity, I continued on SR 28 to SR 375, making a right toward Woodstock as the Catskill peaks beckoned ahead.

Tour **5** *215 miles*

WOODSTOCK • NORTH/SOUTH LAKES HISTORIC SITE • BLACK DOME VALLEY SCENIC DRIVE • HUNTER MOUNTAIN SKI RESORT • SHANDAKEN • PHOENICIA • ARKVILLE • PEPACTON RESERVOIR • ROSCOE • BEAVERKILL DRIVE

A Citadel of Hipness

At the junction of SR 375 and SR 212, I made a left and stopped at the Woodstock Chamber of Commerce Information Center to pick up a tour map of the town. Woodstock (population 7,000) is a two-century-old village sitting in the shadow of the mountains. This famous "Colony of the Arts" was originally a Dutch farming community and still has its village green at the convergence of Rock City, Old Forge, and Tinker streets. Standing proudly, as if guarding the village green, the Dutch Reform Church, built in 1849, is still used today. The white clapboard structure with Ionic columns is typical of the Federal-style architecture of that time, and its simplicity adds to the rustic flavor of the town.

The village green has been Woodstock's traditional town meeting area. During the 1960s, hippies flocked to the town as though on a religious pilgrimage and gathered at the green. That's where I met Jerry, an aging biker, "the Sange," as he called himself. "I'm a leftover '60's hipster on a Harley," he told me. "Yeah, man, Woodstock has changed a lot from those days; they were wild—music and chicks everywhere. Now the music scene has died, a lot of the clubs have closed down, and the town attracts older people and damn yuppies! But it's still cool; check out the Buddhists on the mountain—weird, man."

Woodstock was known as an artists' community long before the legendary 1969 Woodstock Music Festival, which actually took place at the farm of Max Yasgur near Bethel, many miles away from the village. However, as

Watery Cascade.
Lying just a short walk off the highway, Kaaterskill Falls are well worth the time and effort needed to get there.

Art Colony No Longer.
Once a quiet artists' town, modern-day
Woodstock bustles with visitors twenty-
four hours a day.

a result of that festival, the hippies and the curious came to Woodstock in droves, destroying the bucolic atmosphere of the village. Now back to normal, Woodstock remains the home of many craftspeople, artists, musicians, and intellectuals. In a five-block area there are galleries, craft stores, restaurants, sidewalk cafés, clothing boutiques, jewelry stores, and a dozen antique stores.

In 1902 an English Utopian socialist, Ralph Radcliff Whitehead, established Byrdcliff Arts and Crafts Colony, giving rise to Woodstock's first generation of intellectuals. They were attracted to the natural beauty of the area and wanted to escape the dehumanizing aspects of industrialization. The community only lasted a few years but created Woodstock's reputation as a haven for free thinkers, actors, artists, musicians, writers, and educators.

My next stop, the Catskill Center for Photography at 59A Tinker Street, was established in 1977 as a nonprofit arts and educational organization and sponsors various workshops, educational programs, and photographic exhibits. I studied photographs of a cross section of the human condition: a Vietnamese soldier, derelicts, faces in a crowd, tattooed nudes. The building that houses the center was once a sidewalk café where such pop music greats as Joan Baez; Peter, Paul, and Mary; and Bob Dylan gathered to sing.

Following "the Sange's" advice, I drove to the Buddhist monastery and retreat by way of Rock City Road, which turns into Meads Road and leads into the retreat. The road is steep and bumpy, but my small motorhome didn't have any difficulties and large ones shouldn't either. After parking in the designated lot across from the retreat, I walked a few hundred feet down the road to investigate a small chapel.

The Chapel of Christ-on-the-Mount was built in the early 1890s as an Episcopalian chapel for summer visitors. It is still in use today, although practically hidden on the forested hillside. A small wooden cross, formed by two sticks tied together, stands above the fence at the beginning of the trail. The wooden chapel itself is small and well built, with a high-beamed ceiling and seating for approximately seventy-five people.

It became the center of activities for William Henry Francis, a colorful archbishop of the Catholic Church. Father Francis was known as the "hippie priest" because of his following in the 1960s. He's also known for his work with Clarence Darrow on the Scopes Monkey Trial, for which he helped plan strategy, and for his friendships with such diverse celebrities

Petunias by the Bushel.
At a Woodstock farmers' market, potted flowers await inspection by green-thumbed gardeners.

as Carl Sandburg, Frank Lloyd Wright, Franklin Roosevelt, and Bob Dylan. At the age of eighty-five, he helped organize the Woodstock Festival. This unique man, who has enjoyed such a full and exciting life, is still saying mass and lecturing throughout the United States.

Unfortunately, I didn't have the opportunity to talk with Father Francis, so I decided to take a hike to Overlook Mountain and climb the fire tower to see the Green Mountains of Vermont, the Berkshires in Massachusetts, the southern Catskills, and the Hudson River. The easy trail follows a dirt road once used by the wealthy to travel to the Overlook Mountain hotels during the 1870s.

The hotels are gone and the land is now owned by the state, but the views and scenery make it a worthwhile excursion. If you decide to take the hike, be aware that rattlesnakes can be a danger in the area from mid-July to mid-August.

Across the street is the Buddhist monastery and retreat. Buddhism, like Christianity, has many different branches related by a common bond of basic beliefs. This particular sect is Tibetan; their center is called the Karma Triyana Dharmachakra Monastery and Retreat Center. It is the North American seat of His Holiness the Gyalwa Karmapa, head of the Karma Kagyn school of Tibetan Buddhism.

The center, founded in 1978, covers twenty-two mountaintop acres overlooking the Hudson Valley. Its Far Eastern architecture and lovely setting make an unusual stopover. Part of the retreat is housed in the old Meads Hotel, built in 1863 and still reflective of that time. The monastery is still under construction although mostly completed. It will be an exact replica of a Tibetan monastery with hand-crafted construction, frescoes, an eight-foot Buddha statue, and numerous other artistic and religious items necessary in a traditional Far Eastern temple.

Manager Andy Weaver, an American Buddhist, told me the center welcomes nonbelievers who would like to experience the serenity of the retreat and learn something about Buddhist teachings. There are seminars, programs, meditation instructions, and activities throughout the year. Overnight guests can sleep in private or semi-private rooms; Tibetan cuisine is served at mealtimes. It would be a unique way to experience the atmosphere and simplistic life-style of the retreat. I didn't stay, but the quiet solitude and rustic charm of the retreat devoid of many of the technological distractions of the twentieth century has a strong allure.

Back down Meads Road, I made a right onto Glasco Turnpike, and then another right onto Upper Byrdcliff Road. I stopped briefly at the Byrdcliff Theatre, one of the original buildings of the art colony established by Ralph Whitehead in 1902. Today the barn-style wood-frame building, with an intimate seating capacity of approximately 150, is owned by the Woodstock Guild of Craftsmen.

Returning to town, I followed SR 212 east to SR 32 north, a drive with some spectacular views of the Catskills.

At the junction of SR 32 and SR 32A I made a twenty-mile-round-trip detour to visit the Catskill Game Farm and Carson City and Indian Village.

The Catskill Game Farm has been a major attraction in the region for over fifty years. The 140-acre zoo protects over 2,000 animals. A special part of the complex is the petting zoo, where animals roam free. Carson City and Indian Village, two miles north, is one of the largest reproductions of an old western town anywhere in the country today. Stagecoach and train rides, complete with holdups by outlaws; can-can dancers; Indian shows; numerous shootouts; and over sixty carriages and sleighs on display will delight the whole family.

Going back to the junction of SR 32 and SR 32A, I proceeded north to SR 23A east, climbing steeply into Catskill State Park. The road is in good condition but is challenging as it snakes its way into the mountains and climbs over 1,000 feet in a few short miles. There are turnouts, however, and even heavy RVs can make the climb.

The Mists of Kaaterskill Falls

I pulled my motorhome into the parking lot a few hundred feet above the trail head and began the easy, half-mile hike to the misty base of Kaaterskill Falls, actually several falls, with one flowing into another. There is a trail to the top of the falls, but it is far easier to hike to it from North Lake, at the top of the cliff. Feeling refreshed, I pushed onward.

Down from the Misty Mountains.
Wild ferns grow in profusion at the mossy base of Kaaterskill Falls.

Weathered Barn.
An old barn awaits discovery on Scribner Hollow Road between Tannersville and Maplecrest.

Fishing at North/South Lakes

I headed for North Lake Public Campsite, a popular campground where reservations are recommended during the height of the summer season. At the junction of SR 23A and Mountain House Road in Haines Falls, I made a sharp right at the "North Lake" sign; the road to the campground is bumpy and weaving.

Two small lakes at the campground cover eighty-four acres and offer swimming, boating (no motors), and fishing. The campground itself has showers, flush toilets, water, fireplaces, picnic tables, and a dump station, but no hookups. The area was once the location of the famous Catskill Mountain House that catered to wealthy nineteenth-century vacationers and artists, poets, and writers who celebrated the beauty of the region.

Alexander Graham Bell demonstrated his new invention, with much fanfare, by making a phone call from the Mountain House (the first use of a phone in a hotel) to Catskill, New York. Writers Henry James, Mark Twain, and Oscar Wilde and Presidents Ulysses S. Grant, Chester A. Arthur, Grover Cleveland, and Theodore Roosevelt all were guests here. The Mountain

House, with its Greek-revival style and classic portico of thirteen white Corinthian columns, set a style often copied by other resorts.

The Mountain House's hiking trails are state maintained, and the carriage roads are part of New York's horse trail system. There is a plaque marking the site of the hotel, and the location still offers one of the best views on the East Coast.

The warm weather encouraged a swim; afterward I sat on the beach watching some fishermen. The lakes are stocked with fish: New York's hatcheries produce over 300 tons a year, including trout, salmon, walleye, black bass, perch, bullhead, carp, and pickerel. Bass, bullhead, and yellow perch are native to these lakes; fishing licenses can be purchased from the rangers.

A Hike up North Point

Although I've hiked to North Point before, I never tire of the great scenery. There are two routes to the point; the best one is along part of the Escarpment Trail, a twenty-four-mile path from Kaaterskill Falls to SR 23. It's basically an easy hike, with the exception of a few steep climbs, and takes about two to three hours at a leisurely pace. You can rest at various

Mirror, Mirror.
Near the town of Phoenicia, a tiny, unnamed lake mirrors the beauty of the surrounding hardwoods in its still, clear waters.

Wilderness Walks.
A hiker prepares to negotiate one of the many wilderness trails that wind through the Catskills.

overlooks to take in views of North and South lakes, the Catskills, and the Hudson Valley.

One of the nicest spots on the Escarpment Trail is Artist Rock, honoring Thomas Cole (1801–1848), the founder of the Hudson River School (the group of artists who glorified the scenic wonders of the Catskills and the Hudson Valley). Cole, who emigrated to the United States from England at the age of seventeen, achieved international fame for his paintings. He once wrote from Italy, "Neither the Alps, nor Apennines, no, nor Etna itself, have dimmed in my eyes the beauty of our own Catskills. It seems to me that I look on the American scenery, if possible, with increased pleasure. It has its own peculiar charm—something not found elsewhere."

This time I started out on the shorter route, North Lake By-Pass Trail (yellow markers) to Mary's Glen Trail (red markers), which begins just outside the entrance gate and across from Scutt Road. The hike, which is not too difficult, takes about two hours round-trip. If you continue down Scutt Road, you will come to the trail for the easy hike to the top of Kaaterskill Falls.

After struggling up the only steep climb to the top of the rocky, wind-swept peak of North Point, I basked in the 360-degree view: to the east, the Taconic Mountains along the Connecticut and Massachusetts borders with the Hudson River flowing through the farmland of the Hudson Valley in the foreground; and northward, the foothills of the Adirondack Mountains rise silently on the horizon. Gazing west, both North and South lakes float at the base of the mountains. I could see almost the entire length of Escarpment Trail carved into the impressive peaks. A cool evening breeze was blowing, and the last rays of light were slowly fading in the sky. I could see the lights of homes in the valley and even a few flashing glimpses of the campfires encircling the lakes. It is easy to understand how the Indians believed these mountains were the fortress of their "Great Spirit."

Forest Flowers.
Like budding wildflowers, huge Victorian homes dot the thick forests around Tannersville.

Cruising into Black Dome Valley

First thing in the morning I was on my way on SR 23A east to Tannersville, a small western-style town. Several of the buildings have second-floor balconies and wooden facades. A right turn at the light onto SR 23C took me toward Maplecrest. SR 23C is a rough, winding road that will give your motorhome and driving abilities quite a workout. The roads in this area demand slow driving speeds but are adequate for all styles of RVs.

Turning right onto Maplecrest Road, I planned to use an access trail to climb just one of the peaks. I drove down into the small hamlet of Maplecrest, making a right onto Black Dome Valley Road, then proceeding into the horseshoe configuration of mountains that partially encircles the valley. Just before I reached the Batavia Watershed, where one can picnic and swim, a deer shot across the road right in front of me, dashing over a field into the forest. I continued all the way to the end of Black Dome Valley Road, enjoying the views of country homes, the Blackhead Range Mountains, and the peaks of the Escarpment Trail. There is a one-lane bridge with a maximum carrying capacity of two tons just before the parking area.

Downtown Tannersville.
With only a few exceptions, downtown Tannersville looks much as it did half a century ago.

My goal was to hike up Black Dome Mountain. Although a difficult hike because of its steep trail (over 1,800 feet), the shortness of the trail (only 3.6 miles round-trip) makes it accessible to anyone who has hiking experience.

I struggled slowly up the trail for more than an hour before reaching the rocky face of the mountain that is mistakenly confused with the actual summit farther on. The view from this location is spectacular, encompassing large portions of the Catskills and the Hudson River Valley and well worth the effort. After a leisurely snack on the summit, I was anxious to move on to Hunter Mountain and its festival.

Hunter Mountain Ski Resort

I returned the same way but made a right turn off SR 23C onto Scribner Hollow Road to SR 23A and Hunter Mountain. This is a lovely drive through a mountain pass with views of Hunter in the foreground.

Hunter Mountain Ski Resort is one of the most popular vacation areas in the Catskills. During the summer, nonskiers can ride up the mountain on a chairlift to the 3,200-foot summit, the longest and highest lift in the Catskills. The lodge at the summit is open for refreshments, and there are numerous spots to relax, picnic, and hike.

Hunter hosts a variety of ethnic festivals each summer, highlighting various cultures. Varying from year to year, they include the Italian, German Alps, Country Music, National Polka, International Celtic, and the Mountain Eagle Authentic Native American Indian festivals. Schedule information is available at (518) 263-3800.

All the cultural festivals include colorful costumes, foods, music, dances, and souvenirs. The Country Music Festival stars big-name entertainers. During the Native American Festival, I was completely immersed in Indian culture. Listening to the pounding of the drums and the tribal songs and watching the colorful performers from the Iroquois, Algonquin, Navajo, Cherokee, Chippewa, Pueblo, Mohawk, and other tribes dance transported me back in time.

The intricate designs and styles of the authentic Indian crafts, which includes jewelry, carvings, and clothing, are admirable. I enjoyed the art depicting many aspects of Indian history, including colorful paintings of wilderness, hunting scenes, and life on the Great Plains. There was also delicious food to sample, especially Indian fry bread, deep-fried dough coated with honey or powdered sugar, a treat that literally melts in your mouth.

Tantalizing Fare.
Tourists find this traditional Indian fry bread a delightful bonus to a trip to Indian festivals. Everyone seems to love the freshly made treat sold by Indian chefs.

Savage Water and Mystic Mountains

Leaving Hunter, I made a right turn onto CR 83, also called Ski Bowl Road, drove for a short distance, and made another right onto SR 214, which weaves its way to Phoenicia.

Part of Shandaken Township, Phoenicia was settled in 1804 and in its early years was solely dependent on harvesting bark for seven local tanneries. Manufacturers used 20,000 cords of hemlock bark annually, which eventually resulted in the devastation of the forest. Today Phoenicia's main attraction is recreational; there are over 50,000 acres of "forever wild" land to explore, with activities ranging from big-game hunting (bear) to riding river rapids.

Phoenicia sits beside the famous Esopus Creek, noted for its great trout fishing, scenic views, and most recently, tubing. Mountains envelop the village, and the main street is country-quaint with buildings dating back a hundred years. The Phoenicia Inn has been in business since 1853; it's a two-story wooden building with a dining area and bar. After visiting several stores and purchasing some supplies, I drove to my campsite for a restful night before my busy day.

Riding a Wild River

I was back in town the next morning for my tubing adventure. The Town Tinker rents tubes and supplies a shuttle bus at reasonable rates (for reservations or information call (914) 688-5553). The upper river route is approximately four miles long, takes two hours, and has the most challenging rapids. By paying the shuttle fee again at the completion of each trip, you can ride the tube all day. The lower route is shorter and easier; it's a good place to learn because the rapids are few and mild.

Feeling adventuresome, I chose the upper trip and was dropped off at the water-release tunnel several miles west of Phoenicia. The Catskills, besides being a vacation area, are also a massive watershed for New York City, supplying millions of gallons of pure mountain water daily. In fact, if conservationists hadn't fought to preserve the Catskills and save them from exploitation, New York City might not have been able to exist at its current size.

The Shandaken Tunnel is 18¼ miles long, 11½ feet high, and 10¼ feet wide. It passes 2,630 feet below the crest of Balsam Mountain with a carrying capacity of 6,000,000 gallons daily. The tunnel is a major link in the New York City reservoir system, feeding Esopus Creek and then flowing into the Ashokan Reservoir.

As I entered the creek, I was immediately swept away by the current, bouncing along the rapids with the cool river splashing in my face. Waves washed over me, almost overturning the tube, but I fought to stay upright and was moderately successful. I could feel the adrenaline racing through my veins, giving me the extra edge needed to battle the raging water. The river slowed for a while, but soon I was back in the white water again. I became overconfident; the river taught me a lesson by dumping the tube. I held on, pulled by the river's force and power, until I had the opportunity to jump back on.

I floated into Phoenicia in just under two hours, feeling completely rejuvenated. It's an exciting way to spend several hours and relatively safe if you wear a life jacket and are a good swimmer.

Wet, Wild, and Wonderful.
Shooting the rapids of Esopus Creek in an innertube is a favorite for locals and visitors alike.

Above the Clouds on Slide Mountain

From Phoenicia, I headed west on SR 28 to the turnoff to Big Indian Hollow Road (CR 47) that leads to Slide Mountain, the highest peak in the Catskills (4,180 feet). The road is rough with a lot of bumps and uneven pavement but passable for all RVs. The hike up Slide is very popular because of the easy trail, which follows an old bridle path (no longer in use for that purpose) three miles to the summit. The view from Slide is unequaled anywhere in the Catskills—you can see thirty-four of the thirty-five Catskill peaks, as well as a good portion of the Ashokan Reservoir. The drive in and out is approximately twenty miles and the hike takes about three hours round-trip.

A historic marker at the summit honors William Burroughs, who was born more than 150 years ago in nearby Roxbury. This writer, naturalist, and experienced hiker of the Catskills did much to spread his knowledge of the area to the general public. Among his friends were Ralph Waldo Emerson and President Theodore Roosevelt. Although Burroughs traveled worldwide, he always returned to wander among these forests and mountains.

Arkville Depot.
Vintage railroad cars and train memorabilia
are on display at the Arkville Depot.

Old-Time Railroad Days at Arkville

Visiting Arkville gave me the opportunity to relive the Catskill train era.
Early vacationers flocked to the mountains by way of rail, and the Arkville
Depot was one of their destinations. In fact, in 1913, the peak passenger
travel period for the Delaware & Ulster Railroad, they carried 676,000
passengers, making Arkville one of the line's busiest stations.

Today a small portion of that line is back in operation, with plans for
further expansion in the future. Visitors can sit back and relax as they tour
this area of the Catskills by train. This is exactly what I'd planned on doing
by taking the two rides currently available. Unfortunately, a severe spring
flood washed out the Highmount mountain-route ride, which leads back
toward Belleayre State Ski Area off SR 28, and the tracks hadn't been
repaired yet. I had purposely skipped a stop at Belleayre, between Phoenicia and Arkville, because I'd planned on visiting it by train.

Instead I took the tour to Halcottsville, about an hour and fifteen minutes round-trip, with a short stop at Kelly Corners. It was fun riding on a
flatbed car dating back to the 1890s. There are also enclosed cars from the
1920s, but the locomotive is a more recent 1950s' vintage.

For information regarding schedules of the Delaware & Ulster Railroad call (607) 652-2821. Seven towns in two counties are involved in this railroad revival project, and it promises to be a major attraction in the future.

Before leaving Arkville, I made a brief stop at the Erpf Catskill Cultural Center ([914] 586-3326), with its exhibitions of arts, crafts, and Catskill culture and concerts and workshops. I found a large display of beautiful handcrafted quilts quite interesting; some were for sale. I continued along SR 28 to the junction of SR 30 and took SR 30 along the shoreline of the Pepacton Reservoir.

The Pepacton Reservoir/Roscoe/Beaverkill Drive

For eighteen and a half miles the Pepacton Reservoir follows the boundary of Catskills State Park, offering scenic vistas and great fishing. To fish the Pepacton, you need both a New York state and city license. (Contact the Department of Conservation, 50 Wolf Road, Albany, New York 12201, for current requirements to obtain the licenses.)

Pepacton Farmlands.
Fields and farms nudge the river below the massive Pepacton Dam.

Country Village Charm.
In downtown Roscoe, known as the "trout fishing capital of the east," a shopping mall offers everything from ice cream to hand-tied fishing flies.

SR 30 crosses the reservoir about midpoint, where you can see the waters along the mountainous shoreline in both directions. When I reached the junction of SR 30 and SR 206, I decided to go first to the dam, and then backtrack. The view from there is superb, with forested mountains above and farmland spreading out below the dam.

I returned to SR 206 and traveled into Roscoe, named the "Trout Capital of the East" by the Federation of Fly Fishermen due to its close proximity to several of the state's best trout streams. It is also the home of the recently established Catskill Fly Fishing Center, a nonprofit organization dedicated to preserving the heritage of the sport. Plans are under way to build a museum, library, and demonstration and conference center on a thirty-five-acre parcel of land along Willowemac Creek. Currently it occupies a small showroom in town.

Roscoe has the charm of a country village with rural homes and a small, quaint business district. The buildings are over a hundred years old; most

Angler's Paradise.
A fly fisherman plies his art on the quiet, fish-filled waters of the Beaverkill near Roscoe. Considered to be among the best trout streams in America, the river is famous throughout the world.

Trout usually weigh in between six and ten pounds, but every year a few lucky fishermen haul in a few of twenty pounds or more. The Department of Environmental Conservation has a hotline ([518] 891-5413) for the best fishing spots, lure tips, and water conditions.

Beaverkill Bridge.
Built in 1865 and now a popular spot for picnicking, swimming, and fishing, the 118-foot-long Beaverkill Covered Bridge has been carrying traffic across the river for more than 100 years.

are two stories with brick facades, large windows, and heavy wooden doors. There's also a small railroad museum housed in a caboose on Main Street.

I was looking forward to seeing one of Roscoe's nearby historic attractions, the Beaverkill Covered Bridge. I traveled Old Route 17 east, following the sign to the bridge. This is a lovely backcountry drive to the day-use area, and you can swim and picnic at the bridge site or camp along the river at the Beaverkill Public Campground on the opposite side. However, the bridge has a clearance of only six and a half feet, so if your vehicle is higher (and most RVs are), you'll have to call the ranger at (914) 439-4281 or 255-5453, ext. 328 to obtain an alternate route to the campground.

The lattice-style, 118-foot bridge (built in 1865) is a popular spot for trout fishing. I jumped into the river for a quick dip in the cool, clear water. Floating around, listening to the sounds of the rapids downstream, I marveled at the solid wood construction of the old bridge overhead. One side has its original stone base, but the other side has been reconstructed with concrete. Still, with its worn, brown clapboard siding and wooden floor and beams, it maintains its 1800s rural charm.

POINTS OF INTEREST: New York Tour 5

The Catskill Mountains

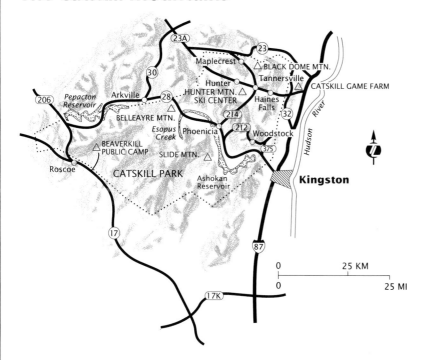

SPECIAL ATTRACTIONS:

Mahayan Temple, Buddhist Retreat with Chinese architecture, year-round, South Cairo; *St. John the Baptist Ukrainian Church,* SR 23A, Jewette Center, 16th-century-style construction, wooden nails, models of historic Ukrainian churches, music and arts center.

OUTFITTERS:

Call of the Wild Guide Service, SR 208, Box 76, Wallkill, 12589 (914) 895-3097.

Catskill Outdoor Adventures, Tremperskill Country Store, Tremperskill Road, CR 1, Andes, 13731 (914) 676-3244.

Tennanah Lake Guide Service, Box 70, Tennanah Lake Road, Roscoe, 12776 (607) 498-5236.

RESTAURANTS:

Woodstock: *Deming Street Restaurant and Cafe* (914) 679-7858; American and international cuisine.

Palenville: *County Line Restaurant,* (518) 678-3101; American cuisine.

Phoenicia: *Cobblestone Restaurant,* (914) 688-5096; German-American cuisine.

Shandaken: *Auberge des 4 Seasons,* (914) 688-2223; French cuisine.

ACCESS: *New York Thruway* to exit 19, Kingston, west on *SR 28.*

INFORMATION: *Delaware County Chamber of Commerce,* 56 Main Street, Delhi, 13753 (607) 746-2281; *Greene County Promotional Department,* Box 527, Catskill, 12414 (518) 943-3223; *Sullivan County Office of Public Information,* County Government Center, Monticello, 12701 (914) 794-3000; *Ulster County Chamber of Commerce,* 7 Albany Avenue, Kingston, 21401 (914) 338-5100; *Appalachian Mountain Club,* McKenley Hollow Road, Oliveria, 12462 (914) 254-4770.

ANNUAL EVENTS:

Woodstock: *Woodstock Artist Association,* arts and crafts displays, June—July; *Woodstock Historical Society,* exhibits, June—July 4.

Hunter: *Summer Ethnic and Country Music festivals,* July—early September.

Phoenicia: *Annual Fair,* United Methodist Church, August.

Livingston Manor: *Shandelee Arts Fair,* July.

MUSEUMS AND GALLERIES:

Woodstock: *Ann Leonard Gallery,* 63 Tinker Street (914) 679-2112, paintings, graphics, sculpture and fine jewelry; *Clouds Gallery,* One Mill Road (914) 679-8155, paintings, pottery, jewelry, and blown glass.

Shandaken: *Blue Barn Art Gallery,* SR 28, (914) 688-7668, Catskills paintings and crafts.

Arkville: *Auto Memories Museum,* County Road 38 (914) 586-4000, May—September; *Erpf Catskill Cultural Center,* SR 28 (914) 586-3326, arts and crafts, Monday—Friday 9 A.M.—5 P.M., Saturday and Sunday 1 P.M.—5 P.M.

The Finger Lakes Area

"Go forth, my children, to the land that I especially prepared for thee and there, all shall find peace and happiness.

Iroquois Indian legend,
about how the Great Spirit led his people to the Finger Lakes area

My attraction to the Finger Lakes region in western-central New York was based on the fame of its diverse geographic beauty: those deep-water lakes, vineyard-covered hillsides, jagged gorges, and numerous waterfalls.

According to Indian legend, the Great Spirit placed his hand upon this land to bless it, leaving behind the imprint of his fingers and thus creating the Finger Lakes. Of course, geologists have a far more mundane explanation. They claim the lakes are the result of two Ice Age glaciers that tore their way across the countryside. The glaciers followed river valleys, carving deeply into them, and when they melted they created a series of six major (and a few minor) lakes.

Indians were the first inhabitants in the area and have a history spanning many centuries. They lived in small agricultural villages and, like the majority of Native Americans in New York, were members of the Iroquois Confederacy. Even though their hegemony was destroyed, their heritage remains.

My first stop was Owego. Holly Dellenger, of the local chamber of commerce, enthusiastically reviewed my tour, offered suggestions, and filled me in on the sights of this national historic district.

Owego was settled in 1787 on a bank overlooking the Susquehanna River. The town developed as a result of its position on the river and dispersed goods produced further north. Lumber, grain, flour, and salt were sent via wagons to Owego, then loaded in boats and shipped to Philadelphia and other ports as far away as Baltimore.

Using the map Holly gave me, I embarked on a walking tour of the town, studying the buildings created in such diverse architectural styles as Greek Revival, Italian Renaissance, and Art Deco (some built prior to the 1860s). The Tioga County Courthouse is a stand-out; it was completed in 1873 in Second Empire style, with four asymmetrical towers, limestone window hoods, and porch columns.

While wandering the streets, I found a marker that related the history of Owego. Like so many other towns in the Finger Lakes area, it was once the site of an Indian village, but was burned in August, 1779, by James Clinton's forces. Clinton, a general in the Continental Army, was en route to join General Sullivan's campaign. Sullivan's forces marched up and down the shorelines of the Finger Lakes, annihilating the Indians, torching their villages, and leaving nothing remaining but the land. From the white man's perspective, his campaign was a great success; he broke the back of the Iroquois Confederacy and secured its land for the new nation.

The Tioga County Historical Museum at 110 Front Street displays many historical artifacts of that era and subsequent decades. This free museum showcases pioneer crafts, Indian artifacts, military exhibits, and primitive portraits.

Tour **6** *218 miles*
*Side trip to Corning and Elmira,
75 miles*

OWEGO • ITHACA • TAUGHANNOCK FALLS STATE PARK • CAYUGA WINE TRAIL • MONTEZUMA NATIONAL WILDLIFE RESERVE • SENECA FALLS • WATERLOO • SAMPSON STATE PARK • WATKINS GLEN • CANANDAIGUA

Riverside Religion.
Nestled on the shore of Lake Van Cleef, the magnificent Trinity Episcopal Church in Seneca Falls combines both Gothic and early English design.

Lovely Susquehanna.
Near Owego, an angler on the
Susquehanna River waits patiently for
the fish to bite.

Into the City of Waterfalls

After leaving Owego, I traveled north on SR 96 through forest and farm-land countryside, making a stop at the Iron Kettle Farm for some sweet corn for dinner. At Candor, I took SR 96B north to Ithaca (population 28,700). Ithaca, called "the biggest little city in the world" because of its cosmopolitan atmosphere and cultural attractions, is home to Cornell University and Ithaca College. Cornell University, overlooking Cayuga Lake and Ithaca, covers a total land area of 13,000 acres. The adjoining Cornell Plantations' 2,800 acres border Cascadilla and Fall Creek gorges, which offers a rugged insight into the geology of the area. The Plantations offer numerous trails, a lake, ponds, woodlands, swamps, an arboretum, and colorful botanical gardens. The nature area is open from dawn to dusk and charges no admission fee.

Walking Ithaca

Ithaca's old downtown area is charming; pleasant streets, attractive build-ings, impressive churches, and a pedestrian mall delight visitors. I parked my motorhome at one of the many parking areas and went for a stroll,

Cornell Campus.
The manicured grounds of Ithaca's Cornell University cover an area of 13,000 acres.

pausing at Ithaca Commons. The commons is bordered by Green, Aurora, Seneca, and Cayuga streets. Most of the buildings have been carefully restored to their original architectural styles. Over 200 shops offer a wide diversity of items for sale.

From the commons, I walked north on Cayuga Street to the Clinton House Historical Society Museum. It wasn't open but its three-story facade, six massive columns, and two balconies were still something to see. Continuing north I came upon the incredibly beautiful First Presbyterian Church, constructed in 1904 of stone, with a bell tower that rises over a hundred feet. Inside I was awed by its colorful stained-glass windows, marble columns, and brass pipe organ that fills the entire area behind the altar. That organ today would cost more than $150,000. The pipes fill an area forty feet wide and thirty feet high. An unusual heat wave made my air-conditioned RV more attractive, so I returned to the road.

A Stop at Buttermilk Falls
Buttermilk Falls State Park, off SR 13 at the southern end of Ithaca, has a stream-fed gorge pool for swimming, campsites, and a total of ten water-falls (there is a vehicle-user fee). Unfortunately, an extensive dry spell had

Buttermilk Falls State Park.
Five hundred feet high, Buttermilk Falls is one of several dramatic waterfalls in the Ithaca region.

turned the thundering power of 500-foot Buttermilk Falls into a small trickle. However, I was still able to enjoy the sight of Pinnacle Rock, a spiral-like rock formation that rises forty feet above the stream, created over the centuries by the erosive power of Buttermilk Creek.

Five miles south of Buttermilk Falls State Park on SR 13 lies the spectacular Robert H. Treman State Park. The park has twelve waterfalls within a three-mile gorge that can be observed by hiking the moderate gorge trail; Lucifer Falls plunges 115 feet down the rugged gorge. After a swim in a stream-fed pool at the base of another waterfall, I returned to Ithaca to travel north on SR 89.

Taughannock Falls State Park

The two-lane road to Taughannock Falls State Park follows the scenic shoreline of Cayuga Lake alongside farms and vineyards. The 215-foot falls plummet through a rock amphitheater with walls reaching 400 feet from

Higher than Niagara.
Located near Cayuga Lake, 215-foot Taughannock Falls is the highest straight-drop waterfall in the northeastern United States.

the base to the top, the highest straight-drop falls in the northeastern United States (higher than Niagara Falls). One way to see this natural wonder is to hike the trail to the base, less than two miles round-trip; or you can drive up the road to an overlook. Doing both is best of all.

A swimming area has ample parking for RVs, along with a marina, sandy beach, picnic area, bathhouse, pavilions, a boat launching and docking area, and playground. But most importantly there is the warm, blue-green water of Cayuga Lake, forty miles long with a maximum depth of 435 feet.

Besides boating and swimming, Cayuga Lake is a great destination for fishermen. Lake, brown, and rainbow trout, northern pike, smallmouth and largemouth bass, land-locked salmon, pickerel, smelt, and panfish are in season year-round. Licenses are available at any town clerk's office. Most of the lakes around here are uncrowded and, as several fishermen attested, very good for fishing. After a relaxing swim, I returned to camp for dinner and an early night's sleep.

Along the Cayuga Wine Trail

I got off to a late start the next morning. It was blazing hot and the sky was hazy. The Cayuga Wine Trail on SR 89 encompasses seven wineries and is an interesting and refreshing way to tour Cayuga Lake. Of course, the temptation is to stop at every winery, but this is dangerous, unless, of course, the driver doesn't drink. If you're traveling with a partner, this is one of those times when you can appreciate having your RV to retire to. Since I was motoring alone, I limited myself to one stop, Hosmer Winery, a very small establishment with less than a hundred acres under cultivation. For a small fee, I sampled seven different wines and received a souvenir Hosmer wine glass. Maren Hosmer, the affable vintner, told me that her

Cayuga Wine Trail.
Scores of wineries lie along Cayuga Lake on the famous Cayuga Wine Trail.

family winery started producing wine in 1985 after New York passed a law allowing small vineyards to produce their own wines. All the ones I sampled were quite good.

Bird Paradise

My next stop on SR 89 was the Montezuma National Wildlife Refuge, covering 6,432 acres and located five miles east of Seneca Falls on SR 5 and US 20. It is both a habitat and resting place for migrating ducks and geese, and home to many other species of birds, small mammals, and deer. You may be able to see some of them from the two observation towers or on the self-guided auto tour over a gravel road. The refuge is open from dawn to dusk. I drove slowly through, stopping every now and again to see if I could spot anything. One of the informative markers tells about the Jesuit missionaries who worked with the Cayuga Indians. Writing about the area in the 1600s, the missionaries noted, "The sunlight over the marsh was actually shut off by the clouds of ducks and geese, and the woods abounded with deer."

I didn't see quite as many birds, but a rather large group of geese seemed to think it was funny to stand in the middle of the road and refuse

Swampy Sanctuary.
Montezuma National Wildlife Refuge is both a permanent habitat and temporary resting place for numerous species of perching birds and migrating waterfowl.

to move. As I inched slowly forward, they hissed their disapproval before finally waddling aside. I stopped halfway through the refuge to look out over the marsh and saw a hawk cruising along on the air currents. Far below, feeding in the marsh were two great blue herons. I never considered myself a birdwatcher, but I could see how one could become enthralled. I cruised on, west on SR 5 (US 20) toward Seneca Falls.

A Hotbed of Radicalism

Seneca Falls (population 7,500) is considered the birthplace of the women's rights movement, which was formed when Elizabeth Cady Stanton, an intelligent, ambitious woman, began to resent the freedom her husband had in comparison to her own. Her life seemed stifled by controls he had never experienced. She saw a relationship between her life and the conditions of all women, and thus concluded that women were unfairly confined by rules and laws enforced socially, legally, and religiously. Stanton and a friend, Jane Hunt, organized the Women's Rights Convention, which was attended by over 300 women and men on July 19 and 20, 1848.

After the convention, the women met again and wrote a Declaration of Sentiments, modeled after the Declaration of Independence. It was signed by sixty-eight women and thirty-two men, but many of the participants refused to sign because it called for the "radical" right to vote for women.

Nevertheless, the convention was considered a success, partly because of the political climate and history of Seneca Falls. Its numerous reformist elements were already in place, including anti-slavery and temperance societies. The Great Western Turnpike bordered Stanton's home and later became Main Street in Seneca Falls. The town was linked with the Erie Canal system in 1828 and the railroad in 1841; consequently, a steady stream of radicals, reformers, and dreamers passed through the town. Some stayed on, while others left only their ideas behind. The result—a town more socially and intellectually progressive than most of the nation.

Seneca Falls honors these women with the Women's Rights National Historic Park. The park has an informative visitor center at 116 Fall Street and owns the Stanton home, Wesleyan Chapel (the site of the convention), and the home of suffragette Amelia Bloomer (originator of bloomers as a style of dress for women). All these places are open to visitors. The National Women's Hall of Fame offers many exhibits about women who have made exceptional contributions in the fields of science, education, business, social welfare, politics, and music.

Leaving the Hall of Fame, I drove along Cayuga Street, a lovely tree-lined road with over fifteen well-preserved Victorian homes. I wound up near Lake Van Cleef and discovered a beautiful old church on the shoreline. The Trinity Episcopal Church was built in 1885 and combines both Gothic and early-English design. Constructed of white stone, it has an impressive display of stained-glass windows and claims to be the most photographed church in the state. After completing my tour of Seneca Falls, I headed west on US 20 in Waterloo.

Well Preserved.
Many of the restored Victorian homes in Seneca Falls are in pristine condition.

Memorial Day Beginnings at Waterloo

Waterloo is the birthplace of the observance of Memorial Day, first held here on May 5, 1866, to honor those killed in the Civil War. During the community-wide observation, all flags were flown at half-mast and, unlike today, all businesses were closed. Waterloo Memorial Park is strewn with historical markers commemorating the war.

If you're interested in the origins of the Church of Latter Day Saints (Mormon), you can take a three-mile side trip south on SR 96 to the Peter Whitmer Farm in Fayette. Here where the church was organized in 1830, you can see a reconstructed 1810 log house, a new Colonial chapel built in 1830s style, and a visitor center; guided tours are available. The four-storied chapel is constructed of white clapboard and sports an impressive tower.

Two miles west of Waterloo on SR 5 and US 20 is the Scythe Tree, a historical curiosity, where local farmboys hung their scythes when they went off to fight in the Civil War, and later World War I.

A Greek Revival Mansion

I traveled west on SR 5 and US 20 from Waterloo until I connected with SR 96A on the eastern shore of Seneca Lake and stopped at the Rose Hill Mansion. Robert S. Rose was a Virginian who came to New York in 1802

Rose Hill.
Built by General William Strong in 1835, the Greek Revival architecture of Rose Hill Mansion near Waterloo illustrates clearly the elegant life-styles of wealthy nineteenth-century New Yorkers.

with his family and slaves and erected a frame house as the seat of his Rose Hill Farm. In 1835, General William K. Strong built the Greek Revival mansion on the land purchased from the Rose family. The mansion has changed hands several times since then and today this elegant estate gives us another rare look at the life-styles of the wealthy in nineteenth-century America. The mansion, furnished in Empire style, has twenty rooms open for viewing. In spite of its massive size, there's a sense of openness as sunlight streams through the large windows, giving the place a cozy feeling. After leaving Rose Hill, I continued south on SR 96A and made camp at Sampson State Park.

Sampson State Park

Sampson State Park is located on the shores of beautiful Seneca Lake, the second largest in the Finger Lakes. Thirty-eight miles long and three miles across, it has a maximum depth of 632 feet, making it one of the deepest lakes in the United States. Mysterious rumbling sounds sometimes come from deep beneath its surface. Legend has it that these weird sounds, called the "death drums" of the Iroquois Indians, are there to remind us that this land was once theirs.

Sampson State Park.
The peaceful RV sites of Sampson State Park beckon to passing travelers.

The lake is great for fishing, with perch, bass, pike, and lake trout (some of which have tipped the scales at twenty pounds or more), accessed by a 126-berth· marina and boat launch. Additional facilities include a tennis court and beach, where I went for a dip. Many people enjoy bike riding on the park's many paved roads. I was curious about the large, flat, grassy sites until I discovered that Sampson was a naval training station during World War II, and later an Air Force training station. Remnants of those bases are visible in some places, and there's a photograph of the park's military tenure in the main office.

The next morning I continued south on SR 96A, enjoying views of the lake and the quiet charm of the farmland I was passing.

A Tour of a Winery

At Ovid, I left SR 96A and continued south to Lodi and the Wagner Vineyards Estate Winery above Seneca Lake, the largest of all the small wineries in the region.

The winery is a third-generation farm that produces 250,000 bottles of wine yearly from its 130 acres of land. Wagner is an estate winery, meaning that all the wine sold under its label is produced exclusively from grapes grown in its own vineyard.

Wine tasting and tours of the facilities are available from April to December. My guide was Sonja Kan Kelfritz, a pleasant and informative local college student. She explained every aspect of wine making, and pointed out the various steps in the process as we toured the winery and wine cellar.

From the winery, I headed toward Watkins Glen on SR 414.

At Watkins Glen

Watkins Glen (population 2,400) is famous for its speedway and its glen. The Watkins Glen International Speedway (off SR 414 south of town in Montour Falls) is a 1,100-acre facility, including a 3.37-mile road-racing track. Even if you're not interested in speedway action, Chequagua Falls, which plunge 165 feet and are illuminated at night, make the short drive there worthwhile.

But Watkins Glen State Park is the most impressive attraction. From its main entrance in the village of Watkins Glen, it stretches west for more than a mile and a half, enclosing eighteen waterfalls, several cascades, amphitheaters, and grottoes within its deep canyon walls. There's a 700-foot drop from the top of the gorge. You can hike through it on an 800-step path, or take a shuttle bus one or both ways.

Entering the gorge, I was pleasantly surprised by the cool temperature; in some places it was twenty degrees cooler than outside the gorge. Its rock walls were formed from sediments that accumulated under water more than 300 million years ago. The gorge itself had its beginnings

Milky Ribbons.
A low camera-shutter speed helped turn these two waterfalls in the Watkins Glen area into milky, white ribbons. On the left is Hector Falls; on the right is an unnamed fall in Watkins Glen State Park.

Watkins Glen.
Winding pathways, steep canyon walls, and
lovely, junglelike scenery, attract hikers and
other visitors to Watkins Glen State Park.

10,000 years ago, at the end of the Ice Age, when a massive glacier retreated and Glen Creek poured down the steep valley. The creek continues
to carve out the gorge even now.

On my hike, I was able to walk behind a waterfall for a look through the
cascading water. A concession stand, picnic area, and comfort station are
located at the top. Descending, I took Indian Trail on the rim, a path
actually used by the Indians when they inhabited the area. I stopped at the
suspension bridge crossing eighty-five feet above the gorge for an
overview.

Natural Sculpture.
More than a mile in length and encompassing eighteen different waterfalls, fairylike Watkins Glen State Park was sculpted by nature during the last Ice Age.

You can camp and swim at the park and, if you visit it at night, you can be treated to Timespell, a light-and-sound show that re-creates the drama of natural and human history from 45 million centuries ago to the present. The park is open from mid-May to mid-October daily from 8 A.M. to 10 P.M. (for additional information call [607] 535-4511). From Watkins Glen you have a choice of continuing the tour north on SR 14A to Canandaigua or taking in a side tour of Corning and Elmira.

A Tour of Two Cities

You can reach Corning (population 13,000) by taking SR 414 south. Corning is the home of the world-famous Corning Glass Center, a unique complex representing the art, science, history, and industry of glass. Interpretive tours, films, galleries, demonstrations, animated exhibits, a gift shop, and artisans at work are just some of its attractions. It is open daily Monday to Saturday 9 A.M. to 5 P.M. and Sunday 12 P.M. to 5 P.M. Call (607) 974-8814 for information.

In Corning's Old City Hall, the Rockwell Museum houses an impressive collection of Western art, including paintings by Charles Russell and Frederic Remington. It's open daily Monday to Friday 9 A.M. to 7 P.M., Saturday 9 A.M. to 5 P.M., and Sunday 12 P.M. to 5 P.M. Call (607) 937-5386 for additional information.

From Corning, you can drive east on SR 17 to Elmira (population 32,000), once the home of Mark Twain. Married to a local woman, he spent twenty summers here writing some of his most famous classics, including *The Adventures of Huckleberry Finn.* Twain is buried at the local Woodlawn Cemetery at 1200 Walnut Street. The Woodlawn National

Giant Eyeball?
Not really. This 200-inch glass disc in the Corning Glass Museum of Science and Industry is one of the largest single pieces of glass on earth.

Where Twain Pondered.
Mark Twain's study now sits on the lawn of the Elmira College campus in the city of Elmira.

Cemetery is also located in Elmira (1825 Davis Street), where the graves of over 3,000 Confederate soldiers who died at the local prison camp can be found.

Several worthwhile museums in Elmira include the National Soaring Museum and the Arnot Art Museum. In addition, one can visit a nature center, many classical and Victorian homes, and the Newton Battlefield Reservation State Park, once the site of a fierce battle between the Continental Army and the Iroquois Indians. The park has camping, hiking, picnicking, and a scenic overlook. I wanted to continue on to Canandaigua, so I headed west on SR 17; north on SR 14 to Watkins Glen, then north on SR 14A.

The Mansions of Canandaigua

Approaching Canandaigua (population 10,400), the road passes through beautiful farmland with green hills of corn and swaying oceans of wheat. At Penn Yan, I took SR 364 to Potter and than SR 247 north to Canandaigua. SR 247 was a bit rough with a lot of recently filled potholes, and it made for a bumpy ride.

Tradition Lives on.
An Amish woman drives a horse-drawn buggy along State Road 364 near the town of Potter. Many of the farms in the area are Amish owned.

Canandaigua was originally an Indian settlement whose name means "the Chosen Place." The original Seneca village was also destroyed by General Sullivan's 1779 campaign. Today, the city sits peacefully on the northern shore of Canandaigua Lake, where visitors can enjoy water sports.

Places to explore in Canandaigua include museums, historic buildings, and interesting shops. The Granger Homestead and Carriage Museum at 295 North Main Street is the restored 1816 Federal-style mansion of Gideon Granger, postmaster general for Presidents Jefferson and Madison. A collection of fifty horse-drawn vehicles spanning the years from 1820 through 1930, period furniture, and household goods used by four generations of Grangers are on display. My favorite attraction in Canandaigua is the Sonnenberg Mansion, built in 1887. Sonnenberg, German for "sunny hill," was the summer home of Frederick and Mary Clark Thompson. Thompson, a New Yorker, was instrumental in establishing the Chase Bank; Mary Clark was the daughter of New York Governor Myron Hooley Clark. Frederick Thompson died in 1899, and Mary lived until 1923, but

Victorian Gardens.
The manicured grounds of the Sonnenberg Mansion in Canadaigua have been described by the Smithsonian Institution as one of the most magnificent late-Victorian gardens ever created in America.

it wasn't until May of 1973 that the forty-room mansion was opened to the public.

The Smithsonian Institution describes the gardens (created by Mary in honor of her husband) as "one of the most magnificent late-Victorian gardens ever created in America," and I could see why. I wandered through the Italian and Rose gardens, sculptured collages of color and design that made me feel as if I were strolling across an artist's canvas. The Rose Garden alone contains over 2,600 rose bushes; there is also the Japanese Hill Garden with a tea house, a greenhouse conservatory, and an arboretum among the nine theme gardens on this fifty-acre estate.

Designed to reflect the grandeur of European nobility, the roomy mansion typified the extravagant attention to detail paid to the homes of the wealthy during the Gilded Age. For information call (716) 394-4922.

I headed west on SR 5 out of Canandaigua, out of the historic and beautiful Finger Lakes region, and on to my next tour, the Western Frontier.

POINTS OF INTEREST: New York Tour 6

The Finger Lakes Area

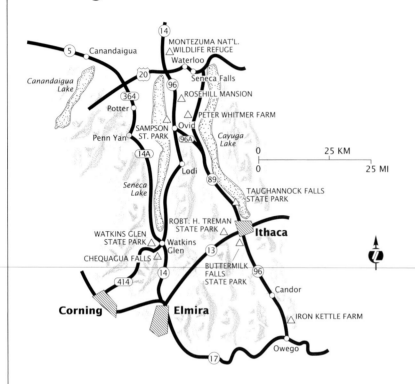

ACCESS: *New York State Highway 17 (Southern Tier Expressway)* to Owego, north on *SR 96* and *SR 96B.*

INFORMATION: *Tioga County Chamber of Commerce,* 188 Front St., Owego, 13827 (607) 687-2020; *Tompkins County Chamber of Commerce,* 122 West Court St., Ithaca, 14850 (607) 273-7080; *Seneca Falls Chamber of Commerce,* Box 294, Seneca Falls, 13148 (315) 568-2906; *Schuyler County Chamber of Commerce,* Watkins Glen, 14981 (607) 535-4300; *Canandaigua Chamber of Commerce,* 3210 Eastern Boulevard, Canandaigua, 14424 (716) 394-4400; *Corning Chamber of Commerce,* 42 East Market Street, Corning, 14830 (607) 936-4686; *Elmira Chamber of Commerce,* 224 Williams St., Elmira, 14901 (607) 734-5137; *Finger Lakes State Parks, Recreation and Historic Preservation Region,* Box 283, R.D. 3, Trumansburg, 14886-0721 (607) 387-7041.

ANNUAL EVENTS:

Owego: *Strawberry Festival,* June.

Ithaca: *Cayuga Wine Trail Barrel Tasting,* May; *Ithaca Festival,* June; *Finger Lakes Antique Show and Sale,* October.

Seneca Falls: *Pageant of the Bands, Cayuga Wine Trail Barrel Tasting,* May.

Elmira: *Chemung Canal Elmira-thon, Chemung County Challenge Triathlon,* June; *Free Spirit Hang-Gliding Festival,* September.

Trumansburg: *Antique Show and Sale,* July; *Taylor Wine Vintage Summer of Song,* August; *Woodcutters Show and Country Fair,* September.

Penn Yan: *Fly In Breakfast,* July; *Buckwheat Harvest Festival,* Sept.

MUSEUMS AND GALLERIES:

Owego: *Tioga County Historical Society Museum,* 110 Front Street (607) 687-2460, Indian artifacts, pioneer crafts, displays, military exhibits, and primitive portraits, year-round, Tuesday–Friday 10 A.M.–4:30 P.M., Saturday and Sunday 1:30–4:30 P.M.; *Tioga Space Gallery,* 72 North Avenue (607) 687-0785, changing exhibits, fine arts and crafts.

Ithaca: *Dewitt Historical Society Museum,* 116 North Cayuga Street (607) 256-3020, Tuesday–Saturday 12:30–5 P.M.; *Hinkley Museum,* 410 East Seneca Street (607) 387-6739, 19th-century art, toys, glassware, and clothing, Tuesday–Saturday 1–4 P.M.

Seneca Falls: *Seneca Falls Historic Society Museum,* 55 Cayuga Street (315) 568-8412, Victorian restoration with period rooms, June–August, Monday–Friday 1–4 P.M.; *Women's Hall of Fame,* 76 Fall Street (315) 568-8060, honors women in all endeavors, Monday–Saturday 10 A.M.–4 P.M., Sunday 12–4 P.M.; *Women's Rights National Historical Park,* 116 Fall Street (315) 568-2991, year-round, Monday–Friday 9 A.M.–5 P.M., June–September, Saturday and Sunday 9 A.M.–5 P.M.

Waterloo: *Memorial Day Museum,* 35 East Main Street (315) 539-2474, items and displays from Civil War to present, Memorial–Labor days, Tuesday –Friday 1:30 to 4 P.M.; *Terwilliger Museum,* 32 Williams Street (315) 539-2474, local history exhibits, Monday 2–5 P.M., Wednesday 7–9 P.M.; *Peter Whitmer Farm Visitors Center,* SR 96 (315) 539-2552, 1810 log house, 1830 chapel, period furnishings, and guided tours, year-round 9 A.M.–9 P.M.

Watkins Glen: *Watkins Glen Racing Museum,* 110 North Franklin Street (607) 535-4204, history, racing cars, memorabilia, Memorial Day–August, daily except Tuesday 1–5 P.M.

Elmira: *Arnot Art Museum,* 235 Lake Street (607) 734-3697, monthly exhibits and world-renowned artists' paintings, year-round Tuesday–Friday 10 A.M.–5 P.M., Saturday 9 A.M.–5 P.M., Sunday 2–5 P.M.; *Chemung County Historical Society Museum,* 415 East Water Street (607) 734-4167, exhibits on Indians, Mark Twain, and local history, year-round, Monday–Friday 9 A.M.–5 P.M., Saturday 1–4 P.M.; *National Soaring Museum,* Harris Hill (607) 734-3128, historic gliders and seaplanes, films and slides, rides, year-round, daily 10 A.M.–5 P.M.

Corning: *Corning Glass Center,* on Centerway (607) 974-8814, history of glass, year-round, daily 9 A.M.–5 P.M.; *Rockwell Gallery,* 23 West Market Street (607) 962-2441, Americana, year-round, Monday–Saturday 9:30 A.M. –5:30 P.M.; *The Rockwell Museum,* Denison Parkway (607) 937-5386, largest collection of Western art in East, year-round, Monday–Saturday 9 A.M.–5 P.M., Sunday 12–5 P.M.

Canandaigua: *Granger Homestead and Carriage Museum,* 295 North Main Street (716) 394-1472, restored mansion, horse-drawn carriages and artifacts, May–October, Tuesday –Saturday 10 A.M.–5 P.M., Sunday 1–5 P.M.; *Ontario County Museum,* 55 North Main Street (716) 394-4975, county history, year-round, Tuesday–Saturday 10 A.M.–5 P.M.; *Sonnenberg Gardens and Mansion,* 151 Charlotte Street (716) 394-4922, guided tours of mansion, gardens, Mid-May–mid-October, daily 9:30 A.M.–5:30 P.M.; *The Wooden Bottle Gallery,* 137 South Main Street (716) 396-2450, local arts and crafts.

SPECIAL ATTRACTIONS:

Owego: *Tioga Central Rail Excursions,* SR 38 (607) 642-5511, May –November, one-and-a-half-hour train rides.

Corning-Elmira: *Schweizer Soaring School,* West Hill Road (607) 739-3821, glider rides, May–September, daily 10 A.M.–6 P.M.

Seneca-Cayuga Barge Canal: Connects both lakes and into the Erie Canal, giving boaters access to the Great Lakes and the Atlantic Ocean, April–November, locks operate 8 A.M.–12 P.M.; maximum vessel size 300 feet long, 15 feet high, with a beam of 43 feet.

RESTAURANTS:

Ithaca: *Ithaca Navigations; M/V Corrine* (607) 272-SAIL, three-hour prime rib dinner cruise on restored vessel; *Valley House,* 801 West Buffalo Street (607) 273-4410; Italian and American cuisine.

Seneca Falls: *Deerhead Inn,* 2254 Lower Lake Road (315) 568-2980; American cuisine.

Watkins Glen: *Savard's Family Restaurant,* 601 North Franklin Street (607) 535-4538; *Glen Motor Inn Wine Country Restaurant,* SR 14 (607) 535-2706; Italian-American cuisine.

Canandaigua: *Crickett's,* 169 South Main Street (716) 394-7990; French cuisine.

LAND OF THE SENECA
The Western Frontier

*God wrought for us this scene beyond compare,
but one man's loving hand protected it and gave it
to his fellow man to share.*

From a poem by Sara Evans Letchworth,
inscribed on a rock at Inspiration Point, Letchworth State Park

T
he "Grand Canyon of the East," Indian reservations, museums, lakes and state parks make up the captivating area in the westernmost section of New York known as the Western Frontier. I continued west on SR 5 from Canandaigua to begin exploring the region.

The Genesee Country Museum

Seeing this rural museum village just as one must have looked in the 1800s, complete with men and women engaged in the activities that residents had to have practiced to survive, is an exciting living-history experience.

Costumed villagers (guides in period dress) greet visitors for a walk back through time at the Genesee Country Museum complex. The nineteenth-century country village is re-created from fifty buildings, original structures dismantled in upstate New York and reconstructed on the museum grounds. Private homes, from log cabins to mansions, farm buildings, and artisans' shops serve as a backdrop for open-hearth cooking, blacksmithing, printing, and crafts demonstrations. The villagers are happy to answer questions about their way of life. There is also a free tractor-drawn trolley for those who don't want to walk the entire complex.

Five fireplaces feed out of a central chimney system in the Amherst Humphrey House (1791), one of the oldest buildings in the complex and typical of the early settlers' homes.

In Thompson's Tavern, museum employee Freida Koenig told me about its history as a shelter and trading post for travelers. Built in Riga, New York, in 1808, the tavern features the large ovens used by villagers to bake their bread. Wooden plank floors and heavy wood-beam ceilings lend an authentic feeling to the two-story Colonial building.

At first glance, the 1870 John Hamilton Villa appears to be the infamous house from Hitchcock's movie classic, *Psycho*. The ornate front porch, period decor, huge windows, eleven-foot ceilings, and the fine craftsmanship of the detailed woodwork all contribute to the sense of the era and life-style of the family who lived here. Next door is the aptly named Octagon House, built in the same year as the Hamilton Villa.

If you're interested in photography, you'll want to stop at George Eastman's boyhood home. The empire-building father of modern photography had his modest beginnings in this 1847 home.

Originally a two-story log house when it was built in 1814, Kieffer's Place was covered with clapboards when milled lumber later became available. The day I visited, a local college student, Andrea Simms, gave a demonstration of basketry. Other locations around the museum complex offer demonstrations of quilting, pottery making, tinsmithing and a variety of the handicrafts necessary to the self-sufficiency of the villagers.

Lovely to Look At.
Red House Lake in Allegany State Park offers passersby a beautiful setting in which to picnic.

Out of the Old South.
Guides wearing period costumes show visitors around the grounds of the Genesee Country Museum near Mumford. One of the more popular attractions here is this magnificent Antebellum mansion.

You can see how they made beer at the brewery and hop house; a brochure highlights great moments in beer history. Artistic interpretations of horse racing, fox hunting, bronco-busting, and wildlife are displayed in the Gallery of Sporting Art. More than forty horse-drawn vehicles can be seen in the carriage barn. Gardens, a picnic area, and snack bar round out the Genesee Country Museum.

You can get information on special events such as the Old Time Fiddlers' Fair, the Morgan Horse Show, and the Highland Gathering by writing to the museum at Flint Hill Road, Mumford, New York 14511, or calling (716) 538-2887.

Now I was off to Geneseo, home to the National Warplane Museum. To reach the site, I traveled south on SR 36, then east on US 20A.

Flying into History

The National Warplane Museum, a private, nonprofit organization dedicated to the restoration of World War II aircraft, displays more than fifteen planes, many of which participate in air shows around the country. During the summer, it hosts an annual air show with more than seventy World War II-vintage aircraft featured. The Curtis P-40 Warhawk was the first U.S. fighter plane to engage in combat against the Japanese and was used in every theater of combat in World War II. The Warhawk could achieve a top speed of 364 mph, carried six 50-caliber machine guns mounted in the wings, and had a 12:1 kill ratio in China.

One of the planes you are actually allowed to enter is the B-17G Flying Fortress, used in combat and for transporting Generals Eisenhower and MacArthur; the smaller planes can only be viewed from the outside.

If you decide to visit the museum, make sure to call first ([716] 243-9887) because at times the planes are away at air shows. Another interesting stop in Geneseo is the Livingston County Historical Museum, a former schoolhouse now home to a variety of historical exhibits.

Grand Canyon of the East

William Pryor Letchworth donated his estate and 1,000 acres of land to help create the park near Mount Morris that bears his name. A successful businessman who felt a sense of duty to help society in many ways, he

Lower Falls.
Cascading over a bedrock bluff, the Genesee River turns to mist at the Lower Falls in Letchworth State Park.

once commented about his mission in life: "For years, I have devoted my whole thought, strength and energy to one thing, business, and have made myself master of that which I undertook to perform. I mean now to cultivate most assiduously the social ties which I have neglected so long fearing they may have become so weakened as to have no influence on my soul."

And cultivate social ties he did! He helped to improve conditions in poorhouses and to better the treatment of the insane and of juvenile offenders. He continually clashed with public officials over his findings and recommendations. Relevant to the park, he dedicated himself to preserving the remnants of the Seneca Nation that had once ruled the region. Letchworth was almost solely responsible for bringing together the descendants of the Great Chiefs of the Six Nations for "The Last Council Fire" held in October, 1872, in the Caneada Council House. (The council house still stands in the park today.)

Attending the council were the grandchildren of such famous Indian chiefs as Red Jacket, Cornplanter, and Joseph Brandt, and of the "White Woman of the Genesee," Mary Jemison. These people had been leaders of the Iroquois who remained loyal to the British. Also present were Presi-

Letchworth Gorge.
The dramatic maw of Letchworth Gorge on the Genesee River dominates Letchworth State Park.

N.Y. State Office of Parks, Genesee State Park Region

dent Millard Fillmore and Letchworth, who was honored at the ceremony with the name Hai-wa-ye-is-tah (the man who always does right).

Letchworth State Park covers 14,340 acres, has a seventeen-mile gorge and three waterfalls. My first stop here was Morris Dam, spanning more than 1,027 feet across the gorge as it holds back the floodwaters of the Genesee River. The dam was built to alleviate damage from the floods that occur on an average of once every seven years. During tropical storm Agnes in June, 1972, water rose to the top of the 790-foot dam and created a lake extending 15 miles upstream through the park.

There are numerous trails throughout the park, rated from easy to moderate. Some have a few steep climbs but for the most part they're easy enough for the entire family. Swimming, picnicking, fishing, and camping are all available. Register early for camping sites; they fill up fast.

I continued on the park road through lovely forested areas, stopping at many of the overlooks within the depths of the gorge. It may be a bit of hyperbole to compare Letchworth State Park with the Grand Canyon, but it is a spectacular sight nonetheless, and having been to both, I wasn't disappointed. It was inspiring to stand on the edge of the cliffs, looking 600 feet down into the rocky canyon at the flowing water of the Genesee. The council grounds sit near the southern entrance of the park.

The White Woman of the Genesee

The house used for the last council of the Six Nations organized by Letchworth is located in Genesee, in the area the Seneca Indians called "The Pleasant Valley." Open for viewing, it is a large, one-story log building with a fireplace. Also located at this site is the grave of Mary Jemison, a local heroine.

Mary Jemison was captured at Marsh Creek, Pennsylvania, in 1755 and carried down the Ohio River by Indians. Subsequently she was adopted by an Indian family that moved to the Genesee River area in 1759. She lived as a Seneca for seventy-five years, and as a result was given the name "The White Woman of the Genesee."

The Roaring Falls of a Country Inn

After leaving the council grounds, I stopped at the Glen Iris Inn, located on a bluff overlooking the canyon and its spectacular upper falls. The inn, originally built in 1828, was acquired by Letchworth in 1859. It's a lovely two-story Colonial structure with white columns, huge windows, and porch, where I sat and listened to the falls. It operates as both an inn and restaurant, and I took the opportunity to sample its cuisine by dining on a delicious meal of rainbow trout.

In the morning, I left the park and traveled south on SR 19A to SR 19 to Belfast. From there, I took SR 305 southwest to SR 17 and headed west. This four-lane highway crosses some of the most picturesque countryside in New York. By the time I arrived at Allegany State Park, the campsites were filled, so I continued west and camped at Highbanks Campsite, owned and operated by the Allegany Indian Reservation.

Fresh from the Chicken.
A highway sign near Allegany State Park advertises fresh farm eggs for sale.

High Bridge.
Visitors can view the Upper Falls and Erie Railroad High Bridge from various vantage points in Letchworth State Park. The High Bridge is now a part of the Conrail System.

G. Lamitina, N.Y. State Office of Parks, Genesee State Park Region

The reservation's 20,469 acres are home to a tribal population of 5,745. Membership in the Seneca Nation is by matrilineal descent; that is, only children of mothers officially enrolled in the tribe are eligible. The Seneca Nation runs quite a few successful businesses, including a sports arena, mini-mart, and bowling alley. Though the campground sits high above the Allegany Reservoir, there is boat access. If you have a boat, the reservoir is a dream come true. Its 13,000 acres of water weave through twenty miles of the Allegheny Mountains in New York and Pennsylvania. Adding to its attractiveness is the fact that there is no development along its shores—ninety-one miles of unspoiled scenic shoreline to explore. Fishing is superb because the reservoir's natural population is further boosted by stocking. Because the waters lie within the reservation, an Indian fishing license is required. Licenses can be obtained at Highbanks Campground on CR 394.

Allegany State Park

After a good night's rest, I made my way east on SR 17 to exit 18 and entered the park, driving along the reservoir on SR 280. The park's 65,000 acres of land have 75 miles of trails, and abundant wildlife: deer, bear, wild turkey, and beaver. At the Quaker Lake section, I turned onto ASP 3 and drove beside the small lake. No motorboats are allowed but canoes and rowboats are; there is also a nice sandy beach for swimming. At the junction of ASP 3 and ASP 1, I took ASP 1 toward Red House Lake. Along the road I was lucky enough to spot a deer as it ran across, and a newly built beaver dam.

The Red House Lake area has swimming, boating, and boat rentals. I continued on ASP 1, taking a short detour on a gravel road to an observation tower. The road requires slow, careful driving, but it is adequate for all

Elegant Alleghenies.
Roadside pullouts in the Allegheny Mountains quite often offer motorists lovely scenic views. This particular vista is of the Upper Allegany Reservoir.

Canoeing Paradise.
Red House Lake in Allegany State Park is a
favorite of canoeists and anglers alike.

RVs. The two-story stone tower rises just high enough to see over the treeline, where I watched a hawk gliding on the air currents. I continued on ASP 1, finishing my drive at Salamanca (population 6,900).

The Indians of Salamanca

Salamanca has the distinction of being the only city east of the Mississippi River located on an Indian reservation. Salamanca didn't become an independent town until 1854; prior to that it was part of Little Valley, called Bucktooth and later, Hemlock. The town changed its name in 1862 to honor Señor Don José Salamanca, a wealthy Spanish banker and a major stockholder in the Erie Railroad. On a visit to the town while on a railroad excursion, the town fathers decided it would be prudent to honor Don José since the town was dependent on the railroad.

The region around Salamanca had been controlled for centuries by the Senecas, members of the powerful Six Nations of the Iroquois Confederacy and descendants of the earliest inhabitants who occupied the region more than 10,000 years ago. They began as hunters and gatherers but evolved into a settled nation whose villages, farms, and laws spread throughout western New York, embracing Iroquois-speaking people in most of Pennsylvania, southern Ontario, and the St. Lawrence area of Canada.

In honor of their great heritage, the Senecas opened the Seneca-Iroquois National Musuem in August of 1977 to give the visitor an overview of the history and the contemporary life and culture of the Indians. Items on display include the actual treaties signed by the Seneca Nation and the United States. You can tour the museum on your own or with an Indian guide. Colorful paintings by Indian artists and a multi-screen slide show detail the life of the Senecas. A museum shop sells books on Indian subjects, as well as carvings, beadwork, postcards, and contemporary Iroquois art. Located on Broad Street Extension, the museum is open Monday to Saturday 10 A.M. to 5 P.M. and Sunday noon to 5 P.M. Call (716) 945-1738 for information.

The American Indian Crafts store at 719 Broad Street sells Indian crafts, jewelry, moccasins, rugs, and many other items. Since the store is owned and operated by Indians, you don't have to pay any sales tax. A few minutes from the store, you'll find the Salamanca cityscape on old Main

Train Buffs Stop Here.
The Railroad Museum in Salamanca displays a fine collection of vintage train artifacts.

Street. This area has been restored and houses over forty shops and restaurants in many historic buildings. A self-guided walking tour reflects Salamanca's history as a lumber and railroad center. Brochures are available at the library at 155 Wildwood Avenue ([716] 945-1890). Leaving Main Street, I headed west on SR 17.

A Visit with the Amish

At Randolph I exited SR 17 and went east on SR 394 for a few minutes before traveling north on SR 241 to Conewango Valley, where I continued north on US 62. In the heart of Amish country, this is one of the prettiest rural areas I've ever motored through. The Amish farms are picture-postcard beautiful with rolling hills of corn, hay, and plowed fields spreading far off into the horizon.

The first twenty-one Amish farmers arrived in the 1950s and bought land from farmers hit by hard times. Since them, approximately 240 families have come to the Leon area, attracted by inexpensive land prices. Because

Simple Transport.
(*Opposite page*) The most modern form of transportation in the land of the Amish is the family horse and buggy. (*Below*) An Amish buggy parked in front of a hand-hewn barn symbolizes the traditional lifestyles of the Conewango Valley.

Amish Country.
Amish farms in the beautiful Conewango
Valley are without electricity, indoor
plumbing, or any other modern
convenience.

they do not use costly modern technology in farming operations, their
expenses are comparatively low, and they have prospered where others
have failed. Driving through the farmland, it's easy to pick out the Amish
farms; they have no electric wires, tractors, or cars.

The Amish are devoutly religious, and their beliefs prohibit the use of
most modern conveniences. They use no electricity, oil, or gas. Cooking
and heating are done by burning wood, and lighting by kerosene lamps.

They cultivate the land "the old-fashioned way," with horse power. Not
all the Amish are farmers. More than fifty Amish shops within the Leon
area (mostly along SR 62) represent the traditional, such as blacksmiths,
bake shops, shoe repair, buggy shop, quilts, and cabinet shops; there is also
one shop producing custom tarps for boats and trailers.

I talked with one Amish family who were in the process of hitching up
their buckboard for an outing. They were gracious enough to spare me
some of their time. John, the father, did most of the talking. He explained
the Amish are almost completely self-sufficient, even to the point of making their own clothes. When I asked if that was difficult, John responded,
"I don't really know, that's women's work," simply relating the facts of
their lives.

John also told me Amish children speak only German until they attend school and then are taught English. Education ends at the eighth grade. I could sense the children becoming restless, so I thanked them for their time and continued on. The Amish have no aversion to tourists as long as their privacy and values are respected. Don't treat them as oddities. By stopping at their shops, you have the opportunity to meet them in a natural situation.

I drove north on US 62 for a few more miles, enjoying the beautiful farms and watching the Amish buckboards clapping down the roads. I began to feel like an alien invader roaring down their bucolic pathways, so I turned around, returning to SR 17, and headed west toward Lake Chautauqua.

Jamestown

Jamestown (population 35,000) was established when James Prendergast received a 1,000-acre tract of land from his brother in 1809 and immediately began capitalizing on the area's natural resources of water power and hardwood forests. By 1827, the town had a population of 400 and

Fenton Historic Center.
A Civil War cannon is but one of the 5,000 artifacts exhibited at the Fenton Historic Center in Jamestown.

began its 125-year fame as a major producer of wood products and furniture.

The city's historic development can be traced by taking separate walking tours of the old north and south sides of town. Fine examples of diverse architectural styles range from Gothic Revival to Art Deco; many commercial and industrial buildings and churches date back to the 1800s. Tour brochures are available at the Fenton Historic Center at 67 Washington Street, (716) 483-7521, housed in the nineteenth-century mansion of former New York Governor Reuben Fenton. During the Civil War, it was the headquarters for the Grand Army of the Republic. Today, its exhibits and collections include nearly 5,000 local items from the 1800s, 2,000 books and manuscripts, and almost 10,000 photographs, daguerreotypes, maps, and genealogical records. Folk art, Indian artifacts, agricultural and textile implements are on display. I enjoyed the center and recommend stopping in for a visit.

For shopping, the Jamestown business area offers stores and specialty shops selling everything from books to locally manufactured furniture. A wide selection of restaurants caters to a variety of tastes, some with dancing and entertainment. Jamestown has two resident theater companies and extensive programs of gallery showings, ballet, art, films, and music. After touring some of the city's many attractions, I drove west along the shore of Lake Chautauqua on SR 394.

On Lake Chautauqua

Jamestown sits on the tip of beautiful twenty-two-mile Lake Chautauqua, famous for its swimming, boating, and most of all, fishing opportunities. The lake's walleyes and smallmouth bass have a well-earned reputation for size and quality. But the most famous fish of Chautauqua is the tiger muskellunge; this prized "fighting" fish can grow to over forty pounds!

A few miles west of Jamestown is the Chautauqua Institution, a community founded in 1874 and devoted to education, creativity, and the arts. Originally an educational center for Sunday-school teachers, it evolved over the years into a world-famous cultural, entertainment, religious, and educational center. The Institution is actually a self-contained shoreline community on 700 acres, with nineteenth-century houses, wooden walkways, a theater, churches, and guest inns. I left my motorhome at a large parking area near the entrance and leisurely strolled through the grounds, enjoying the views of the lake and the community. Victorian cottages only a few yards apart line the narrow, wooded streets that slope down to the water.

It's a pleasure just to walk around the Institution, and the community hosts a wealth of professional programs—plays, operas, and symphony concerts, as well as lecture series on religious and philosophical topics. When I was there, speakers included former Attorney General Edwin Meese, former Virginia Governor Charles Robb, and former *Ms.* magazine Editor Suzanne Braun Levine.

Educational Center.
The world-famous Chautauqua Institution is a teaching center devoted to education, creativity, and the arts.

I continued west/northwest on SR 394 to Mayville for a cruise on Lake Chautauqua. I relaxed in the cool afternoon breezes aboard the *Chautauqua Belle,* a replica of a nineteenth-century paddlewheel steamboat. Reservations can be made by calling (716) 753-7823. A replica of a sixteenth-century ship, the *Sea Lion,* is scheduled to begin operation in the near future, after fifteen years of research and construction; call (716) 753-2403 for information. The yacht *Gadfly* is also available for a one-and-a-quarter-hour cruise.

As my New York tour came to an end, I realized New York truly is an "Empire State" with a fascinating history that spans thousands of years. I couldn't help but wonder how different that history might have been had the Europeans arrived a few centuries later. Would the powerful and advanced Iroquois Confederacy have continued to prosper and increase their might to the point where their hegemony over New York couldn't have been challenged and, therefore, their land not taken from them? Or was

Tall Ship.
The *Sea Lion*, a replica of a sixteenth-century sailing ship, is moored in the small town of Mayville.

their demise inevitable due to the technological inferiority of their weapons?

I realized these questions could never be answered. But there was one thing I knew for certain: The Iroquois would have been pleased with the massive areas of land that have been preserved in their natural state and deemed "forever wild," allowing people to enjoy the impressive beauty of the Empire State for "as long as the sun shines and the rivers flow."

I recalled the Indian legend about how the Great Spirit created the Finger Lakes and thought that the story could apply to all of New York that I had seen. The state is indeed "blessed with beauty and abundance."

POINTS OF INTEREST: New York Tour 7

The Western Frontier

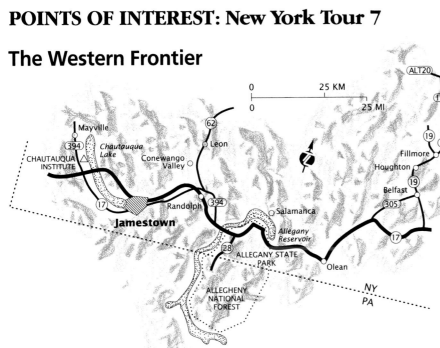

ACCESS: *New York Thruway (90) to* exit 47, south on *SR 19*, east on *SR 5.*

INFORMATION: *Genesee State Park and Recreation Region,* Letchworth State Park, Castile, 14427 (716) 493-2611; *Allegany State Park,* RD 1, Salamanca, 14779 (716) 354-2182/2545; *Cattaraugus-Allegany County Tourist Bureau,* 636 Wildwood Avenue, Salamanca, 14779 (716) 945-2034; *Jamestown Area Chamber of Commerce,* 101 West 5th Street, Jamestown, 14702 (716) 484-1101.

ANNUAL EVENTS:

Mumford: *Genesee Country Museum,* numerous special events, May through October.

Geneseo: *1941 Warbirds Air Show,* August.

Salamanca: *Trout Derby,* April; *Miller High Lite Regatta,* Allegany Indian Reservation, June; *Allegany Indian Fair,* September; *Seneca Nation Indian Christmas Bazaar,* December.

Jamestown: *Festival,* July; *Sculptures and People Fair,* July and August.

Chautauqua: *Craft and Alliance Show,* July and August; *Challenge Triathlon,* September.

MUSEUMS AND GALLERIES:

Mumford: *Genesee Country Museum,* Flint Hill Road (716) 538-2887, 19th-century homes, businesses, artifacts, art, crafts, and exhibits, May 9–October 18, daily 10 A.M.–5 P.M.

Geneseo: *National Warplane Museum,* Big Tree Lane, off SR 63 (716) 243-9887, World War II and Korean War planes and artifacts, year-round, Monday–Friday 9 A.M.–5 P.M., Saturday and Sunday 10 A.M.–6 P.M.; *Livingston County Historic Museum,* 30 Center Street (716) 226-8694, Indian relics, costumes, Victorian room, and war relics, May 1–November 1, Thursday and Sunday 1–5 P.M. or by appointment.

Castile: *Letchworth State Park,* (716) 493-2611, pioneer and Indian history museum, exhibits, artifacts, clothes, and photographs, year-round 10 A.M.–5 P.M.

Salamanca: *Rail Museum,* 170 Main Street (716) 945-3313, year-round, Monday–Saturday 10 A.M.–5 P.M., Sunday 12–5 P.M.; *Seneca-Iroquois National Museum,* SR 17.

Jamestown: *Art Gallery,* James Prendergast Library, 509 Cherry Street (716) 484-7135, paintings, artifacts, local history, Memorial Day–Labor Day 9 A.M.–5 P.M., September–May, Monday–Friday 9 A.M.–9 P.M., Saturday 9 A.M.–5:30 P.M.; *The Heritage Museum of Childhood,* displays and locations change, call (716) 484-1101 for information.

Mayville: *Depot Museum,* SR 394, changing exhibits, July–September 3, Saturday and Sunday, 1–5 P.M.

Olean: *Friedsam Memorial Library,* St. Bonaventure University, 14778, (716) 375-2323, major collection of masterpieces by Rubens, Rembrandt, Winslow Homer, and others, call for hours.

SPECIAL ATTRACTIONS:

Jamestown Flying Service, scenic flights, Chautauqua County Airport, Jamestown, (716) 483-0111.

OUTFITTERS:

Jim Kenealy, RD 1 Morner Road, P.O. Box 174, Rensselaer, 12144 (518) 465-8222.

Frenchman Guide Service, Box 231, North Maple Street, Ashville, 14710 (716) 763-8296.

RESTAURANTS:

Mount Morris: *The Genesee River Hotel,* SR 36 (716) 658-2929; Italian-American cuisine.

Letchworth State Park: *Glen Iris Inn* (716) 493-2622; American cuisine.

Belfast: *Jean's Truck Stop,* "Home of the Herbie Burger," SRs 19 and 305; country diner (no phone).

Jamestown: *Ulla's Restaurant,* Commons Mall, East Third Street, (716) 483-3884; Scandinavian foods.

Index

Page numbers in **boldface** refer to illustrations in the text.

Tours

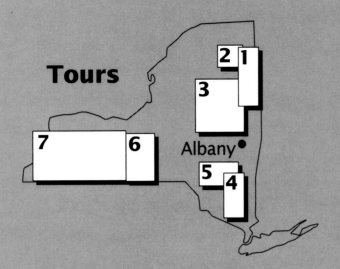

Albany

7 6

Niagara
Falls

Oswe

Lockport

104

Rochester

63

490   490   Newark

14

190   Tonawanda

Batavia   20   90   Geneva   Aubur

Buffalo   20   Canandaigua   Sene

400   77   Falls

Seneca   ALT   Canandaigua   Seneca   Ca

20   Lake   Lake

219   390

19   Dansville   89

Dunkirk   16   39

90   70   Itha

Fredonia   Gowanda   17   Bath

394   62   Hornell   14   13

Chautauqua   Allegany   17

Lake   Indian Res.   36   Corning

17   219   Olean   417   Wellsville   417   15   Elmi

Jamestown

0   50 MI

0   100 KM

New York